The Customer-Centered Enterprise

The Customer-Centered Enterprise

How IBM and Other World-Class Companies Achieve Extraordinary Results by Putting Customers First

Harvey Thompson

McGraw-Hill

New York   San Francisco   Washington, D.C.   Auckland   Bogotá
Caracas   Lisbon   London   Madrid   Mexico City   Milan
Montreal   New Delhi   San Juan   Singapore
Sydney   Tokyo   Toronto

Library of Congress Cataloging-in-Publication Data applied for.

McGraw-Hill

*A Division of The **McGraw·Hill** Companies*

1 2 3 4 5 6 7 8 9 0   DOC/DOC   9 0 9 8 7 6 5 4 3 2 1 0 9

ISBN 0-07-135210-4

Printed and bound by R. R. Donnelley & Sons.

This publication is designed to provide accurate and authoritative information in regard to the subject matter covered. It is sold with the understanding that the publisher is not engaged in rendering legal, accounting, or other professional service. If legal advice or other expert assistance is required, the services of a competent professional person should be sought.

   —From a declaration of principles jointly adopted by a committee of the American Bar Association and a committee of publishers.

This book is printed on recycled, acid-free paper containing a minimum of 50% recycled, de-inked fiber.

McGraw-Hill books are available at special discounts to use as premiums and sales promotions, or for use in corporate training programs. For more information, please write to the Director of Special Sales, McGraw-Hill, 11 West 19th Street, New York, NY 10011. Or contact your local bookstore.

For Rosalyn

Contents

Contents

Preface

One of the biggest problems facing CEOs today is how to continuously attract customers and attain growth, often in an environment where products and prices among competitors are steadily moving closer together. Traditional bases for differentiation, such as product features or cost, are becoming less tangible and senior management is forced to look for new ways to stay attractive to a target market. CEOs and senior management across virtually all geographic and industry lines have now put the word "customer" into their formal business vision and mission statements, and all are searching for a vehicle to operationalize that "customer focused" vision, differentiate themselves and compete upon value delivered by processes and services.

—FROM HARVEY THOMPSON
AND PROFESSOR MERLIN STONE,
"CLOSE TO THE CUSTOMER
— CUSTOMER VALUE MANAGEMENT"

The purpose of this book is to provide senior management with the means to take a vision (for a company, a business unit, or a business process) of being "Number 1 in the Eyes of Our Customers" and to make it a reality.

What keeps you awake at night? IBM conducted global research to identify, in effect, "What will keep CEOs and senior management awake at night as we begin the twenty-first century?" The overwhelming response was a passion to become closer to the customer and to achieve a more customer-oriented culture and business vision. It seems that no matter what the industry or geographic locale, managing customer relationships (attracting, developing, and retaining customers) is the single most powerful issue for businesses today, and it is expected to be the biggest issue tomorrow. With the emergence of the Internet, this will become even more pronounced as customers' expectations are dynamically reset and increased almost daily. As industry boundaries are redefined and creative new e-business value propositions are introduced, companies will experience relentless pressure to understand and meet their customers' rapidly changing needs.

The desire to become customer-centric and the preferred provider of products and services is familiar territory. Over the past several years, as a management consultant for IBM, I have worked with the CEOs and top-tier management of major corporations throughout the world. Their companies were in diverse industries, such as automotive, insurance, banking and financial services, retail, distribution, public and private utilities, petrochemicals, manufacturing, and federal, state, and local public agencies. What impressed me most was that, although they represented a broad array and variety of personalities, management styles, and business environments, they had much in common. Virtually all shared a mission or vision statement with a focus on the customer, but most lacked a methodical approach and an operational framework to accomplish that mission or vision.

They repeatedly stated that a customer-focused strategy was one of their most serious and troublesome challenges. They spoke of an inability to develop and then institutionalize or operationalize such a strategy enterprisewide and of the difficulty to migrate to a customer-focused culture. Understanding the customer and managing the full relationship (end to end, across multiple channels and touch points) were felt to be critical issues. Time and again, CEOs and senior managers said that customer-facing processes represent the greatest opportunity to differentiate a business and to attract and retain market share.

As customer centered as these comments seemed, they were from executives whose offices typically featured a chart on the wall proclaiming the company's product distribution channel strategies rather than channel strategies to provide customer-defined, ideal access to the company and its products. If the objective is to bring an enterprise closer to the customer and to have a customer-focused culture, which phrase communicates a better channel strategy:

distribution channels for products or

ideal access channels to those products for the customers?

Which one would your customers believe is better?

Each CEO articulated a vision with an outside-in point of view to be perceived by customers as ideal. But the strategy to attain it reflected traditional inside-out thinking (to distribute or push their products and services toward customers). In other words, there was a disconnect between the pictures on the wall and the narrative. They were incredibly inconsistent. And I found this to be a common pattern that went beyond the channels to virtually all of the customer interactions with each company's people, processes, and services. Their expressed (outside-in) customer-focused visions were not in alignment with the plans, programs, and strategies generated by traditional (inside-out) management methods and approaches. As my wife is fond of reminding me, "We human beings are not yet perfected." Apparently that also applies to business management, especially on the critical topic of making a customer-centered vision a reality. In today's environment, good managers with good intentions are simply not good enough. New and innovative management skills and approaches are required. Without such innovation, CEOs will have sleepless nights well into the new millennium.

The development of new approaches to align a dynamic marketplace with the institutional structure and culture of a business has been the focus of extensive IBM research, development, and management attention. For the past several years, the corporation has undergone a transformation, unprecedented in scope and scale, to become horizontally (process) managed and customer centered. We, too, have a vision and mission to be the premier provider of (in our case, technology-related) products and services to our customers. And when we began the journey to fulfill that vision, we also found an absence of methods in the existing management sciences to address the issues.

The business literature of the time emphasized process management and reengineering simply as a means to reduce internal costs and increase productivity, and our early efforts were not immune to that thinking.

However, as our process work matured, our focus moved from an internal view of improvements to an external one to create exceptional value for our customers. Initially, my job was to define, document, reengineer, and manage the continuous improvement of customer-facing business processes for IBM in the United States. This evolved to a corporate mission to develop creative new techniques that used the voice of the customer (a customer-defined vision) to drive business improvements and process engineering based on what the customers themselves valued. Ultimately, as we gained experience, these approaches further evolved to become global client consulting.

The benefits of combining business process management (continuous process improvement) and customer-focused process reengineering were quickly apparent. They resulted in improved delivery of value to our customers and to our clients' customers, and they greatly increased our internal management effectiveness and flexibility. For example, prior to introducing these process concepts into the IBM management system, it would have been much more difficult to restructure several large divisions with product-focused missions into smaller, more customer-focused organizations. Major companies that do not have cross-functional business process management can envision ideal new organization structures, but they often lack the flexibility to implement them. The horizontal flow of business activities can be so poorly understood and documented that if a portion of that workflow (say, a person or a division of the company) were to be removed as the result of reorganization, the work might actually stop. Potentially, no one beyond that (now missing) individual or division would know where the workflow came from or went to. In other words, if you lost the elevator operators, you couldn't run the elevators. The connections between the various vertical functions, or "floors" of the business, are often held together by the information in people's heads, not by institutionalized knowledge and formal documented processes. This exposure can have a chilling effect on organizational creativity and performance.

I wasn't an elevator operator, but I was in the right spot when IBM realized it needed to identify, document, and improve the company's cross-functional processes so that vertical organizations might be rearranged or realigned for effectiveness without damaging the business.

To fulfill the vision would require new techniques and approaches. We conducted research to identify and integrate the very best available methodologies worldwide. Where no such frameworks existed, we created them. For instance, during our early work, there were few examples of how to conduct competitive benchmarking for nonmanufacturing processes (e.g., ways to use primary or secondary research to identify world-class business process practices). So we visited practitioners of manufacturing benchmarking at other companies, and we met with leading academics. Then we developed our own nonmanufacturing approaches to identify the best practices for customer-facing processes. After testing these with benchmarking partners, such as Xerox and Hewlett-Packard, we were invited to share these approaches at international forums on benchmarking, where they were recognized as "best practices" in their own right. The same is true of many of the topics discussed in this book.

It has been an exciting time that has resulted in the development and formalization of major new customer-centered management frameworks and ultimately the writing of this book. In the chapters that follow, we share what we have learned from our research and associations with some of the finest minds and thought leaders in business and academia. We cover best practices that will help your firm become customer focused and customer preferred. We review the art and science of attracting and retaining loyal customers. New, differentiating best ways to be close to the customer are identified and documented. These include customer-visioning methods that use customer-defined needs, wants, and values to design new business capabilities and infrastructure. Ongoing business process management system frameworks are also covered to make these approaches part of your business fabric. The term applied collectively to these disciplines to become customer centered and the ideal provider of customer-defined value is customer value management (CVM).

Harvey Thompson

The Customer-Centered Enterprise

Introduction:

Ready, Aim...No, Really Aim

On a recent business trip to Atlanta, I used my Hertz gold card account to reserve a car. It was typical Atlanta weather when I arrived—nearly 100°F and humid. As any global traveler and road warrior knows, what can go wrong will go wrong, so I wasn't expecting exceptional service when I picked up my rental car.

I couldn't have been more wrong. There at the Hertz lot was my name in lights—"Welcome Harvey Thompson," it said—right above "my car." The engine was running and the car's air conditioner was cranking away. All I had to do was drop my bag in the luggage compartment and drive off in complete comfort. At that moment, in my mind, the name Hertz was also up in lights.

Then I arrived at my hotel. As a Platinum-level member of the hotel's customer loyalty program, I had stayed at many of their locations in the past and was looking forward to relaxing in my room. Finding a parking place took several minutes, however, and there was a line at check-in. So I waited. And fumed. And jingled the change in my pockets, impatiently. Eventually, I made a caustic remark to the person in line behind me that this hotel apparently never had anyone stay there before. We must have been the first customers they had ever dealt with. Why else, I reasoned, were they unable to check people in more efficiently—like, like...like the rental car company I had just visited?!

At that moment, the hotel was not aware of the level of dissatisfaction that a valued customer was experiencing. Worse, they were not aware that my expectations for service from them had been reset not by their competitors, but by a rental car company. And this phenomenon occurs thousands of times a day, worldwide, across millions of customers, and for all industries, not just hotels and rental cars. The rush to attract and retain customers by providing differentiating service is creating an upward spiral of expectations that effectively raises the bar for everyone. This puts pressure on all businesses to stay in tune with changing customer needs and wants and to ensure alignment between what customers want and the ability of the business to deliver.

To be fair, the hotel has and deserves a stellar customer-service reputation. It uses one of the most sophisticated reservations and check-in systems in the hospitality business and, overall, is a big user of leading-edge technology. But all this did little good when I and a group of other business travelers had to wait to check into a room. For many of us (e.g., Hertz gold card holders), our expectations had been set by totally different industries, which had effectively eliminated customer lines or queues to obtain services.

But how could the hotel know that I just had a great experience with Hertz? Or whether the fellow behind me had received terrific service from an airline and would now also have a higher standard of service in mind when approaching the counter at the hotel? Or maybe he was delighted with a hotel he stayed at the day before. How could the hotel, or any business for that matter, track and respond to the rapidly changing expectations of so many diverse customers?

And which of their customers' opinions should count most from the hotel's standpoint? For example, I travel on business for a large corporation. It is safe to say that I represent a very large customer grouping or segment. Maybe the fellow in line behind me does, too! How are the expectations of such major customer segments set? How often do they change? Which of their expectations or needs impact bottom-line business results? How can the company identify and weave those changing needs into the plethora of process interactions and management activities that represent how that company does business?

To be successful in today's environment of rapidly changing customer needs and perceptions of value, these questions must be answered, and the answers must be institutionalized and used to prioritize and drive business investment and improvements. In other words, a means must be found to incorporate the customers' viewpoint into every business's management system.

Customer value management (CVM) has become a leading approach to attract market share and customer loyalty by making the customer's view an integral part of the business design. It is the means by which companies can balance the demand for service, even create that demand, with an infrastructure that (a) is customer-centered, (b) delivers increased productivity, and (c) benefits the company's bottom line. Successful CVM boils down to understanding the complex system wherein customer expectations are set and devising ways to meet those expectations consistently.

Companies today must continuously monitor and maintain an alignment between their customers' dynamic vision of ideal value delivery and the capabilities of the business to deliver that value. This is done by identifying and targeting desired customers and then having those very customers develop a vision of receiving ideal delivery of value from each interaction with your company. The company can then develop a strategy to have the specific business capabilities and enabling infrastructure to deliver the ideal value. This engineering of business capabilities with a focus on customer-envisioned value can be accomplished via an IBM framework for customer value management. The approach is not a project, but an ongoing management system to consistently monitor changes in what your customers demand and to maintain an alignment with the business infrastructure and capabilities to meet those changing demands.

Customer value management provides the basis to become customer centered and attain growth by enabling an organization to be "Number 1 in the eyes of its customers." This book describes what CVM is, how it is deployed, and presents case examples to illustrate its key principles. Ideally, after reading it, you'll find out who is setting your company's name up in lights and who's grumbling while waiting in line. You will be able to act on that knowledge to drive business improvement and growth.

To test your current CVM capabilities, each of the subsequent chapters in the book concludes with a set of management issues and strategic questions that your organization must be able to answer to become ideally customer centered.

1

Customer Value Management

Achieving the Vision

Vision without action is a daydream.
Action without vision is a nightmare.
JAPANESE PROVERB

Virtually every corporation you can think of has a vision and a strategy to achieve it. I can't tell you what each of them says, but most share the same theme: "Where do we want to be in three to five years, and how are we going to get there?" To get there, many of these companies have also consistently tried the same things. Both their efforts and results have a lot in common. For starters, in the late 1980s many corporations began downsizing in order to boost profits. Critics said such moves amounted to little more than trying to save your way to profitability. Business results said the same: Surveys of companies that downsized revealed that fewer than half had experienced improved operating profits, very few had actually increased productivity, and in many instances, the stock price (shareholder value) of downsized companies was significantly lower than that of similar firms which had not downsized.

Point taken. So corporations did more than simply cut back. In the early 1990s, companies began to reorganize or reengineer themselves to increase productivity. That can be an easy target for criticism, too. If you've reorganized, fine. But for whom? And why? Who's actually going to buy your product or service once you've finished laying everyone off and reengineering? And so on.

So corporations went on reinventing themselves: creating product segmented groups, industry-specific this and niche-marketing that, reorganizing and re-reorganizing in an endless search for the "silver bullet" that would bring success. Library shelves were loaded with books about boosting business and making the company more (usually price or cost) competitive.

But what always struck me was the one thing missing from all of these tomes on business advice: the concept—indeed, the very presence of the word—*customer*. Best-selling books at that time did not focus on the customer, much less feature the word in their titles. It seemed that the customer was a relatively unimportant element in the formula for business success.

That isn't surprising. Incorporating the word *customer* into the vision or mission statements of business organizations has been a fairly recent phenomenon, especially when viewed in the context of the 100-plus years since the Industrial Revolution. The customer has not traditionally appeared in a company's stated reasons for being; normally, the shareholders occupied that lofty space (e.g., "To provide our shareholders with industry-leading value and returns."). Until the 1990s, the world of business was typically characterized by overdemand, and customers were often literally relegated to stand in line while eagerly purchasing all the products and services that could be manufactured and delivered.

No more. In today's environment, the world can be characterized by overcapacity, and customers have become kings and queens. They have taken on new importance as the focal point for business, as seen on the banner of corporate stockholder reports and mission and vision statements (e.g., "Our vision is to be the premier provider of [insert product or service] to our customers.") (Figure 1-1).

The old management philosophy, "If you build it, they will come," is being replaced by a new executive order, "Find out what they want and give it to them." There is empirical research today that such customer-focused firms simply make more money. A multiindustry study by the Wharton School, for example, found that a reduction in annual customer attrition of only 5 to 10 percentage points can actually increase a company's profits by 25 to 75 percent, depending on the industry. When you consider that many American businesses report annual customer attrition rates approaching 20 percent, the potential profit leverage from becoming customer centered is immense, and that doesn't include the benefits of attracting customers from competitors and growing market share. To remain

The Customer-Centered Enterprise Vision

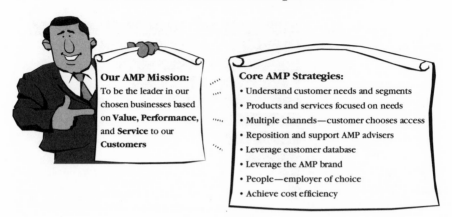

Our AMP Mission:
To be the leader in our chosen businesses based on **Value, Performance,** and **Service** to our **Customers**

Core AMP Strategies:
- Understand customer needs and segments
- Products and services focused on needs
- Multiple channels—customer chooses access
- Reposition and support AMP advisers
- Leverage customer database
- Leverage the AMP brand
- People—employer of choice
- Achieve cost efficiency

Figure 1-1 The new era: Making the customer the design point for business vision (*Source: AMP Financial Services, Sydney, Australia*)

successful today, the theme for a business's vision and strategy must change from, "Where do *we* want to be in five years?" to, "Where do our *customers* want us to be, and how do we get there?"

"Great idea," you may be saying. "Now how do we do it?" Unfortunately, another thing shared by many CEOs, company presidents, COOs, CFOs, and CIOs (all of the CXXs) is a marked absence of an approach to put such a customer-focused vision into real action. Management's ability to develop a vision has often exceeded its grasp in terms of being able to implement the realities of the required changes down to the desk level. However, implementing change is vital if a company is going to make the customer the design point for all business activities, behaviors, and metrics of success. In other words: Good idea; poor execution. This common problem is raised repeatedly in our discussions with senior managers globally. And when it is introduced during talks on "Becoming Customer Centric" at professional conferences, one can feel the audiences palpably react and lean forward in their chairs. Everyone, it seems, shares this concern, as indicated by results from a study sponsored by IBM of global senior executives to identify the things they felt would be most important to their business after the year 2000 (Figure 1-2).

Customer value management (CVM) represents the very best practices used today by IBM and client executives worldwide to

Customer Relationships: The #1 Source of Competitive Advantage

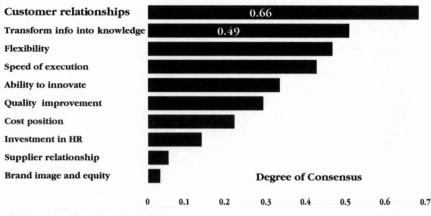

Figure 1-2 The top issue: Becoming a customer-centered enterprise

attain their visions of finding out what customers want and giving it to them. Customer value management provides a rational set of techniques, methodologies, and strategies to weave the needs and wants of customers into the key process designs and management activities of a corporation. Refined extensively at IBM and leading client corporations, these approaches to drive customer loyalty and growth are becoming the pathway to corporate renewal and change, displacing traditional reengineering and quality management mindsets.

Customer value management is a way of doing business. Employed correctly, it can help a business enterprise create and sustain differentiating value. In other words, it is a vehicle to understand what your customers or clients want of you and how you can go about aligning your business to deliver that product or service consistently.

But if CVM is the result of lessons learned and if it can be explained in such simple terms, why don't more companies practice it? Why don't more companies listen to what kind of a business their customers want them to be and then go ahead and be that kind of company? Or why don't they make informed judgments to not become that kind of company, but only where the identified customer vision does not make business sense? The obvious answer is that CVM is a lot harder to implement than to understand.

Easy to Say; Hard to Do

It's easier said than done. Why? Just as there are common themes among many companies' strategic mission or vision statements, there are also some very common reasons they are difficult to implement. We address these reasons and how to work through them in this book.

To begin, implementing a customer-focused vision requires a major shift in most companies' strategic thinking, often including a radical move from product or price as the basis for competition to process or service value. An accelerating phenomenon among many industries is that the products from one company increasingly resemble those that are offered by most of the competitors. Former bases of differentiation, such as product features, quality, or price, are becoming less and less discernible as new technologies become widely available and quickly turn what were perceived as exclusive products into commodities. Overnight delivery services get that package into someone's hands within 24 hours. Airline tickets from New York to Miami cost pretty much the same, regardless of the air carrier (although, curiously, each seat may have significantly different fares on the same airplane). Most new cars get great mileage and many receive somebody's award for engineering excellence. The result is that customers aren't lining up to buy any given product type from a single dominant company. Why? Because virtually the same product can be obtained elsewhere at a comparable price.

As a result, many businesses today are moving from product- or price-based competition to service and value as their competitive point of differentiation. By focusing on not only the Service department or function ("big S" Service) but also on the service element of every department's interactions with customers ("little s" service), a firm can create and add value to the relationship, differentiate itself, and be more attractive to customers. That's why airlines and car rental companies offer tiered customer service (Bronze, Silver, Gold, Platinum) to retain high-value customers and why car manufacturers now focus so much energy on making sure their dealerships provide the best possible customer service without limiting it to the customer service department. That's the first issue: changing strategy from product- and price-based competition to service and the value provided by customer-facing processes.

The second major difficulty is that a shift to competing with customer-facing processes requires a new customer-orientation for company goals, metrics, organization structure, management systems, and procedures. This shift may literally take a cultural transformation to effectively align the business processes with an external customer viewpoint (i.e., seeing the business in terms of access channels for customers instead of distribution channels for products). The recent phenomenon of adding the word *customer* to today's business vision and mission statements is the first step in this direction. It provides an organizationwide signal, both to employees and to shareholders, of the importance of the new strategic direction, which virtually all will find easy to say but hard to do.

Aligning with the customers' viewpoint introduces a third reason CVM can be very difficult to implement: Many companies simply do not have good input from their customers, and almost all do not have ideally actionable input. IBM found in the 1980s and early 1990s that having good people with good intentions was not enough. The ability to execute a customer-focused vision and strategy is proportional to the presence or absence of actionable customer information. This, in turn, is often linked to something else we commonly see in companies: millions of dollars wasted on misguided, irrelevant research such as poorly constructed customer opinion studies and satisfaction surveys. The results of these expensive surveys are usually found at the bottom of two-drawer file cabinets. They should be serving as actionable components and drivers of the firm's business strategy and investment plans.

The automobile company example in Chapter 2 illustrates this point. For years, the organization surveyed its customers on items such as their satisfaction with the service area cleanliness and waiting room facilities. Unfortunately, these questions did not measure how likely customers were to buy another car from that manufacturer. This type of customer research is typical, but hardly relevant or actionable. Customer value management provides a systematic approach to acquire a customer view that is highly actionable and linked to buyer behavior. Instead of asking about the waiting room, the company could have asked customers what factors make them likely to buy additional vehicles and what factors deter them. Conducting subsequent satisfaction surveys regarding those specific factors provides actionable information the manufacturer can act on in order to build and retain customer loyalty.

Another vision attainment problem we frequently find across many industries is initiative gridlock. The CEO of a major global company recently described this type of traffic jam on the program-du-jour highway. He said his company has scores of well-intentioned employees, programs, and initiatives bumping against one another, frequently at cross-purposes, and with no apparent common progress for the overall business. This environment is often the result of a strong sense of urgency and business direction that have been passed down the organization ladder coupled with an absence of methodical approaches to prioritize and implement improvements across multiple business units, organizations, functions, processes, and geographic locations. Each of these entities may, in turn, have its own unique cultures, management systems, measures and metrics of success, incentives, financial resources, ways of doing things, customer sets, and prior experiences or successes with change. Add to the mix that each department may also have its own understanding of what the business direction means in the first place, and the result is often initiative gridlock.

Each organization, for example, may strive to fulfill a corporate mandate to cut costs by taking actions that pass costs on to other departments and collectively increase total company cost. Similarly, quests for growth often result in uncoordinated initiatives company-wide, which step on one another and actually result in customer confusion. When the business direction contains both cost reduction and growth directives, it can result in initiative conflict, making it difficult for a management team to rationally prioritize and allocate scarce resources, such as information technology (I/T) skills or investment dollars. That is because each manager aggressively contends for his or her fair share, which typically means 100 percent. Properly implemented, CVM provides an enterprise with a rational framework for prioritizing, aligning, and linking business initiatives—effectively breaking the gridlock—by using the customer viewpoint as the common denominator and tiebreaker. The voice of the customer sets the priorities for business initiatives and, ultimately, how your resources are allocated.

And finally, to complete our list of why achieving the vision is so difficult: Historical silos of vertical organization structure, management systems, measurements, incentives, and information management are major inhibitors to achieving a customer-focused vision. Silos naturally exist when the way of doing business, the infrastructure, information, and virtually every aspect of how work is performed are unique, and proprietary, from one entity in a business enterprise to another. The result is that functions such as human resources, marketing, shipping, receiving, and other departments fail to communicate or interact in the optimal way. Because any given business process flows across multiple functions, the process is repeatedly compromised as each function seeks to meet its own needs rather than those of the whole enterprise or, most important, the needs of the customer.

Much has been written about the need to overcome the siloization of businesses, but little has apparently been identified to effectively eliminate it. At its best, siloization can result in suboptimization at the silo or individual function level as opportunities are missed to subsume the interest of the silo in order to attain a greater overall benefit to the parent company or organization. At its worst, silo thinking can result in a toxic culture and in behaviors that are far more serious than mere inefficiency or ineffectiveness caused by people bumping into one another. That is, not only do different departments fail to interact, but they may also actively and aggressively avoid cooperating to maximize their own results.

As one executive of a major technology firm put it, "What we have in this company are warring tribes and guerrilla warfare...faction against faction. Each one is flying its own flag and attacking or defending itself against the other." But even where behaviors are not so visibly contentious, the natural effects of a traditional, functionally aligned (silo) organization tend to work against the overall company or business unit vision of being customer focused.

As an example, when IBM began looking at business process management as a way to ensure high customer satisfaction, silos had a natural countereffect. On the one hand, both the business process managers and I/T applications owners were incented to develop creative automated means of satisfying customer needs with efficient new processes. On the other hand, the I/T operations managers were measured on system availability and resisted taking the systems down to test or install the resulting new applications. One I/T operation initially put into effect a practice that this could be done once a month so as not to impact their own performance indicators. This type of silo suboptimization occurs countless times in all major enterprises. Announcing a new vision or business direction to be customer focused or process centric does not change this mentality the next day. As a result, when a business has a vision of being customer centric or undertakes a strategy to compete on service and customer value delivery, silos become the enemy. The delivery of customer-defined benefit or value is almost always the result of cross-functional, cross-silo activities (or horizontal, cross-functional processes). This requires breaking down silo walls, paving over castle moats, and the efficient, effective, horizontal coordination of all resources and activities to optimally meet targeted end customers' requirements.

For every given customer-desired outcome, the full value chain relating to how a customer perceives and obtains value from the company must be identified and managed (possibly redesigned or reengineered) as a single entity with the customer as the focal point. Customers' needs and definitions of ideal value delivery must serve as the design points for the business and value chain capabilities, and the customers' perceptions of performance must become the final arbiter or ultimate metric of success. In the end, internal performance measures, management systems, incentives, and rewards must be aligned and linked horizontally to the desired external customer need or want. And that requires addressing all of the aforementioned issues, common to most senior management, which make achieving a customer-focused vision difficult.

Understanding and properly implementing CVM will help CEOs and their management teams address each of the issues covered in this chapter. By the time you finish this book, you will have a clear understanding of rational, methodical, and world-class CVM approaches to:

1. Develop and implement a business vision to become customer centered, that is:
   - "Grow the business by attracting market share."
   - "Be Number 1 in the eyes of our customers."
   - "Be the premier provider of [product or service X]."

2. Implement an operational strategy to differentiate and compete on service and value to customers, not merely on products and price.
   - Create value at touchpoints to attract and retain customers.

- Harvest each interaction to improve targeting and personalize service.
- Provide value to customers commensurate with their value to the firm.

3. Understand what drives customers' loyalty and buying behavior and give it to them!
   - Fulfill your customers' vision of an ideal you.
   - Make the customer a key part of your business.
   - Make your business a key part of the customer.

How to Get There: The Customer Value Management Approach

We begin with an overview of the CVM framework. Figure 1-3 depicts the starting point for a CVM analysis—an outside-in customer vision of the firm as their ideal provider.

Becoming customer centered with CVM starts by identifying the target customers and securing their vision of the ideal outcomes from doing business with the company. This includes:

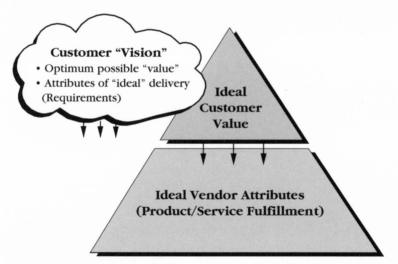

Figure 1-3 The customer view: Ideal value delivery (© Copyright IBM, 1999)

- How the customer perceives value or benefit from interactions with company products, services, and processes (the value proposition at each interaction).

- What the minimum level of value *must be* to retain customers.

- What the optimum level of value *could be* that the customer can envision.

- What the attributes of an ideal vendor and of ideal value delivery *would be* to influence buyer behavior, loyalty, and growth.

The Rest of the Book

The book explores in detail how to obtain such a highly actionable customer view as well as how to convert that into a rational set of business improvement priorities and actions. The underlying concepts that support the overall CVM approach are explained in Chapter 2:

- Chapter 2. Visioning: Customer As Design Point for Business Engineering

In Chapters 3, 4, 5, and 6, we cover how to populate the top of the CVM pyramid (Ideal Customer Value in Figure 1-4) with an actionable customer vision to drive business improvement and investment decisions:

- Chapter 3. Focus: The Top of the CVM Pyramid: Whose View Counts?

- Chapter 4. Scope: Selecting Highest Leverage Customer Interactions

- Chapter 5. Value: Identifying Actionable High-Leverage Customer Needs

- Chapter 6. Prioritization: Making Investment Decisions Based on Buying Behavior

Then, we explore new approaches to define the bottom elements of the pyramid (Essential Process Capabilities and Enabling Infrastructure in Figure 1-4) required to fulfill the customers' view of ideal value delivery:

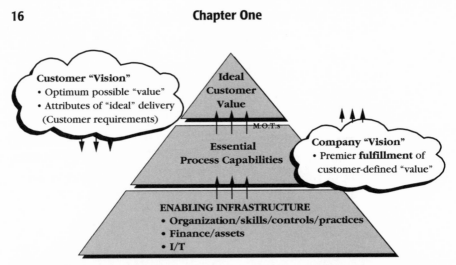

Figure 1-4 The company view: Aligning your business design with customer value (envisioning the new value-delivery processes) (© Copyright IBM, 1999)

- Chapter 7. Design: Envisioning "Ideal" Customer-Defined Business Capabilities

The customer-defined vision of ideal outcomes from interactions with company processes (Figure 1-3) becomes the basis to envision the actual business capabilities and infrastructure required to deliver those outcomes (Figure 1-4). Benchmarking and technology scans also identify the best examples of those capabilities that may be emerging in other industries. These are used to assess the company's existing processes, capabilities, and infrastructure and to isolate the missing elements and define the transformation that will be needed to acquire them (Figure 1-5).

The capability "gaps" provide design points for process improvement (or for engineering fundamentally new processes) and the basis for a rational work plan of specific projects to acquire the missing enabling infrastructure (Figure 1-5).

Finally, the realities of an ongoing journey must be dealt with. The strength of CVM's approach is that it ties your business design with the needs of high-leverage customer sets. However, it must also become an integral part of your ongoing management system. A major exposure of aligning your business with customers is that customers change who they are, what they want, and how they perceive competitive alternatives. If you use CVM to engineer a set of business

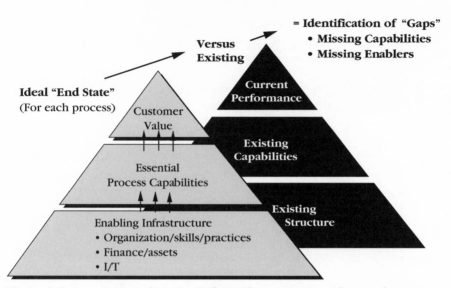

Figure 1-5 Assessment and action: Defining the requirements for transformation (© Copyright IBM, 1999)

capabilities as a one-time event, then your company will have perfect alignment with its market on the first day of the new process. On the following day, however, you will be one day out of synch with changing customer needs, newly introduced competitive alternatives, and new perceptions of your company as a qualified provider. Attaining a customer-defined vision of your company as the preferred provider is a dynamic moving target. Each day, new standards are being set by the Hertzes, Marriotts, and Singapore Airlines of the world as they strive to differentiate themselves by providing ideal value at each interaction with their customers, thus raising the performance expectations bar when those customers come to you.

As a result, the coverage of this topic cannot be considered complete without a discussion of how to institutionalize the CVM approach into your business. An ongoing process is required to continuously monitor the marketplace, identify newly emerging segments or changing customer needs, maintain and update the customer-defined vision for the business, and identify new investments required to address new capabilities gaps. Such a process both inputs and drives the management system to prioritize customer-focused investments and business-improvement actions.

The concluding chapters address managing and sustaining the transformation required to monitor gaps and maintain alignment with changing customer needs:

- Chapter 8. Implementation: Balancing Actions, Strategy, and Change Holistically
- Chapter 9. Maintenance: Sustaining CVM, Always
- Chapter 10. The Journey: A Customer-Focused Evolution

EXERCISE
Applying CVM to Your Business

Management Issues

Your products and prices are becoming progressively similar to those of competitors. How can you compete? How might you differentiate your business, attract share, and grow by becoming a more customer-centered organization?

1. Customer in the vision
   - What is your business mission and vision statement?
   - Is the "customer" prominently featured? How? For example, is it your vision or mission to become the preferred provider in the eyes of the customer?
   - Do you traditionally compete on product? On price as a low-cost provider? How might the value or benefits from your processes and services augment your core products?
   - How might your current or future high-value customers receive benefits during interactions with you and be further attracted by your process and service value?
   - Who is setting your customers' expectations?

2. Customer in the execution
   - How can siloization and initiative gridlock be overcome by making the customer the key arbiter for business priorities?
   - Are a customer-focused vision or mission and a strategy to attain it clearly defined and communicated throughout the organization and down to desk level?
   - Are business functions aligned into cross-functional customer value chains (horizontal business processes)?
   - Are activities and workflows synchronized and managed horizontally to attain customer-defined outcomes?
   - Do your goals, objectives, measurements, and incentives link to the customers' priorities and measure value chain performance?
   - How do you monitor changes in customers' needs and maintain your ability to meet them?

2

Visioning

Customer As Design Point for Business Engineering

Prior to battle, planning is everything.
Once the battle begins, however...
DWIGHT D. EISENHOWER

In 1995 I was having discussions with the then-chief executive officer of a major European automobile manufacturer. He was attempting to change radically the culture of the firm, making it more customer focused. His goal was to align all products, services, processes, and employees with the wants and needs of a particular highly valued target customer segment.

IBM had developed a plan to enable the automobile company to better understand its customers' needs in a highly actionable manner: the significant interactions between the company and the targeted customer segment would be examined; the customers themselves would develop a vision of receiving ideal value at each interaction; their needs would be prioritized and performance issues would be identified. This would pinpoint areas where action must be taken to close any performance gaps with competition; business capabilities and infrastructure would be reengineered where needed to ensure alignment with customers' needs. In other words, the car maker was embarking on a plan to leverage customer value management (CVM). But planning isn't enough because becoming truly customer focused means you must develop an ability to relentlessly take an outside-in view of your business. And that is much harder than it sounds.

The CEO, nevertheless, was exuberant with the plan. We were right on the money, he said. He also added, "I have a vision for this company that I think is very important to communicate to every employee worldwide." With a flourish, he concluded, "My vision is that *selling a car is the beginning of a lifelong relationship.*"

Here's where consultants earn their pay. One of my Nordic colleagues took a deep breath and told him he was off the mark by a long shot.

Why? Because the vision he had stated was not customer focused at all; it was internally focused and expressed an inside-out view. Nowhere in the statement—selling a car is the beginning of a lifelong relationship—did the customer's view of the business appear. Such a vision communicated the continuation of internal metrics of success (selling) as being paramount to the employees and to the customers. Worse still, strategies, plans, programs, and priorities to make the business customer centered were based on an inside-out perspective on the relationship with customers. It assumed that the customer thinks the way you think.

We explained to the CEO and management team that getting an outside-in viewpoint meant they had to take the customer's perspective continuously on all interactions with the business. To do this, the CEO and everyone in the company had to look at the company from the outside, begin calling things by what customers call them, and using customers' terms, not the company's. This would establish the mindset that a business relationship with their company actually begins with the customer.

Indeed, the new company vision, we said, should not be selling a car is the beginning of a lifelong relationship. It must instead become *buying* a car is the beginning of a lifelong relationship. The CEO agreed, adding, "We have a lot of work ahead of us."

Getting on Target: Not an Easy Task

This automobile company is certainly not alone when it comes to missing the mark while trying to come up with a company vision. Scores of companies have put hundreds of person-hours into developing internally focused visions that do not reflect the customer's view.

But why is it so difficult for an organization to become customer focused? Why do so many firms proclaim a vision, mission, or strategy to be the best in the eyes of their customers, yet fail to meet that standard? Chapter 1 provided an initial list of significant common issues. To understand those better, however, one must look to the roots of how management has been practiced traditionally, because rooted in this tradition is an almost genetically encoded mindset that drives management behavior today. If not understood, this mindset is very likely to unravel our best efforts to create customer-focused change. It will stubbornly, and often invisibly, reset the organization back onto the original course.

Good Intentions Paving the Way to Failure

The European automobile company's problem, indeed virtually any company's problem, is that it relied almost solely on the guidance of good managers with excellent intentions. Sounds contradictory, doesn't it? How can having smart managers with only the best intentions be wrong? Put simply, they're wrong because business managers have been conditioned to approach business management issues in a certain way—inside-out—for the good of the business. As a result, the behavior and thought patterns of successful managers reflect a certain prejudice or historical foundation in how they analyze things, make trade-offs, and reach decisions.

In his book *Reengineering the Corporation* Michael Hammer likened automating old and outdated business processes to paving cow paths for high-performance sports cars. In a way, managers are taught, with all good intentions, to do the same thing when managing a business. The methods they learn to apply in business school often perpetuate outmoded business practices.

Figure 2-1 explains this fundamental problem. Traditional management disciplines have focused on where we want to be and how to get there. This process, often called *management by objectives,* has been a core principle taught for decades in introductory business classes. Simply stated, it means that we must decide what we want to attain, set the objectives that will signal our arrival at the desired state, and then manage the business to attain that state. As

traditionally applied, management by objectives has become the
inside-out model that drives organizational behavior. At this point, it
has been effectively programmed into the decision-making DNA of
business school graduates. When applied to the current business
environment, it often unravels newly set, externally focused business
directions or initiatives.

In this typical scenario, the business carefully manages the attainment of its agreed-to objectives, such as market share, costs, product
defects, cycle time, and of course, customer satisfaction. ("See?" some
would say. "They are including the customer in this formula!" No,
they're not, and I'll provide some insight on why this is a fallacy in a
moment.) Unfortunately, this almost always means objectives we
have set for ourselves rather than objectives set for us by our customers, who are the reason for the existence of our products, services, and processes. The company identifies performance gaps and
then subjects the manageable elements of the business (how work
gets done, how people are organized and managed, how resources
and assets are utilized) to the current-era management tools du jour
for refinement and improvement. Again, the business is simply applying analytical management tools to attain its own internally set business objectives and metrics (Figure 2-1).

**Managing by Objectives: Where do WE want to be
and what must we do to get there?**

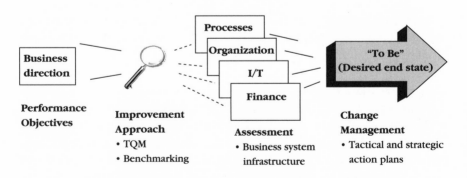

Result = An internally focused business strategy

Figure 2-1 The old paradigm: Management 101 (© Copyright IBM, 1999)

The company then develops strategies and tactics to improve its processes, organization, and resources in a way that helps attain the desired end state. Unfortunately, time and again, the actual bottom-line results are off the mark.

Management 101, or managing by objectives as traditionally practiced, results in an internally focused company. ("Where do we want to be and what must we do to get there?") Missing from this scenario is actionable input from customers. The company defines the objectives.

The result, assuming it is successfully executed, is that the company may indeed hit the specific bull's-eye objectives that they have defined but miss the intended overriding target, such as a goal of increased external customer satisfaction, loyalty, and market share. One reason for this is that the internal focus of the business strategy and objectives may be totally transparent to the management team. After all, they will reason, things such as improved market share and increased customer satisfaction are ranked at the top of our "managing by objectives." How could improving customer satisfaction be considered an internally focused objective? Here are a few examples that provided valuable insights early on in our journey.

Utility Company: Great Execution, Wrong Vision. A utility company's TQM-era experience continues to be one of the best examples of good managers doing the wrong things really well. The company won a coveted Japanese award for quality. (If the Malcolm Baldrige Award is considered the penultimate American quality achievement, then this award was considered by many to be the equivalent in global recognition.) In winning the award, the firm's excellent management team was driven down a strictly defined path, including regular reviews ("inquisitions" in the words of one surviving senior manager) by prominent Japanese academics and leaders in the field of quality. Reportedly, there were no acceptable excuses for missing the objectives that top management had established to qualify for the award; the pressure to perform was intense and relentless.

An important element of the award was the requirement for customer focus, and the management team relentlessly pursued that end. Other than rates, they reasoned, the customers would most value relief from lengthy power outages. Living in an area that often has inclement weather, customers were experiencing frequent power failures, many of which lasted for several minutes. It seemed logical to the managers, considering the complaints that accompanied tropical storms, that minimizing the length of a power failure would be perceived as valuable by customers. Therefore, having established their customer focus and agreeing to specific improvement objectives, the company methodically executed total quality management (TQM) disciplines to remove the root causes contributing to the average customer downtime.

Their efforts paid off handsomely; over a period of months, the average time per outage was dramatically reduced from several minutes to only a few seconds. Other business objectives were similarly targeted and attained. Ultimately, after years of such concentrated efforts, the firm received its reward and recognition—the much-coveted award for quality. The CEO declared victory and subsequently retired.

Yet while the company was attaining their customer-focused objectives, actual customer satisfaction was, amazingly, on the decline. Customers were not impressed that a power outage now lasted only a few seconds compared to a few minutes. Regardless of the duration, customers still had to reset every clock, VCR, and microwave in their households after each outage. If they were working in an office, they still had to retrieve and reconstruct lost computer files, reset their voice mail greetings, and reset all the clocks there, too. In other words, minimizing the amount of time a power failure lasts was far less important to customers than avoiding a power failure in the first place. The company had successfully implemented plans to attain an objective that they believed to be customer focused, but which had little value as actually perceived by customers! In the case of their power outage objective, it was the number of outages, not the duration, that was the metric most used by customers to determine quality, and every time they had to reset their clocks, they were reminded of this lack of value. And the phenomenon was, no doubt, repeated across other such "customer-centered" measurements.

On assuming his responsibilities, the new CEO received a surprise. The public regulatory agency, even while the utility was accepting its award, had continued to receive customer complaints on topics such as power failures and was now challenging the company to demonstrate that it was providing sufficient value to its customers to warrant its rate structure. The CEO subsequently removed much of the top management team, with the admonition that while spending the past two to three years focused internally, in pursuit of an award, they had taken their eyes off of the customer.

Hotel Chain: Great Vision, No Execution. On the other hand, we observed that some firms knew exactly what their customers wanted, but failed to give it to them. Once, while traveling for personal pleasure, I experienced a situation that could be considered the direct opposite of the utility company. I was visiting my son while he was away at college and decided to stay at a medium-priced hotel that's part of a national chain. This hotel chain had a national advertising campaign wherein it promised guests that its hotels would have no surprises, or in effect, zero defects in their product. The concept of zero defects is easy to understand in manufacturing. But what did that same concept mean for the lodging and hospitality industry? It certainly didn't mean what I experienced.

At check-in they had no record of my reservation, but they did have a room available, possibly because they lost someone else's reservation. In my room, I found a nonworking television set (and I really wanted to watch a football game that day), and the lights in the entry area did not work. However, there on that little round table that is in all hotel rooms—a table that is too small to be of any real functional use—was a tent card that advertised this hotel chain's commitment to no surprises during a traveler's stay. I did what any traveler would do: I brought the tent card and news of the apparent mismatch between the service promise and the delivery to the attention of the hotel manager. The young man I met was extremely apologetic and explained that the company really did want to deliver on the promise of no surprises and zero defects, but all that existed at that point was the promise. The company simply did not have the internal infrastructure to deliver on the promise.

He went on to say that the hotel chain had decided to target and attract the highly lucrative business traveler market segment. A very good idea. Their next step was to develop a customer-focused vision of the company that would appeal to the values of the business traveler segment. Another very good idea. Their final step was to promote that vision or image in national publications read by business travelers. This was not a good idea because in doing so they had actually raised the expectations of their target customer segment without also raising, aligning, and linking their business capabilities to execute the vision.

Note: The hotel experience occurred several years ago. Judging from more recent television advertisements, the company is now getting it right. The chain has introduced television commercials informing their customers that they are investing in renovating their infrastructure to deliver an improved level of customer value and experience.

The commercials are aligning their customers' expectations with their actual capabilities and infrastructure by conditioning the customer to expect to experience work in process. By displaying images of customers staying in hotels where renovations are going on around them, the company is setting customer expectations, which will match their actual environment and capability to deliver.

The experiences of the utility company and the hotel chain exemplified how firms with excellent managers can have truly good intentions but fall far short of the desired results.

In the case of the utility company, the management team was quite adept at executing a plan (i.e., managing by objectives), and they clearly understood that those objectives should contain a customer focus. However, at the time, the company lacked a methodical approach to capture actionable, customer-defined metrics of success, as well as to use that external viewpoint to effectively establish business strategy, goals, objectives, and performance assessment. In other words, the company could do things in a world-class, award-winning manner, but from a customer value and loyalty management standpoint, it lacked the means to know exactly what it should be doing.

In contrast, the hotel chain had a good view of what was important to customers, but did not invest in the capabilities and infrastructure to deliver on those things. Their efforts lacked a true customer focus.

CVM was subsequently developed to enable management teams to do both: get an actionable customer view and take the actions that result in increased customer satisfaction, loyalty, and market share.

Obtaining the Customer Vision

At this point, you may be thinking that it should be obvious that the best way to understand the customer view is to do what thousands of companies have done for years: survey their customers. Ask them what they think of the service or product the company delivers to make sure that their expectations are being met. But simply asking such questions is not enough. As you will find in this and subsequent chapters, surveys have serious limitations as a means of identifying customer requirements.

Automobile Company and IBM: Asking Lots of Questions About the Wrong Things. An American luxury car manufacturer and IBM are two examples of organizations that have gone to great lengths to obtain customer input. Both firms routinely survey their customers to obtain a measurement of customer satisfaction. The automobile company has traditionally attained consistently high satisfaction responses to its customer surveys. The organization's management was recognized when it won a major award for excellence in service quality attainment and customer focus. However, while car owners were responding favorably to the firm's satisfaction surveys, they were also defecting to Lexus and Infiniti. What was the problem?

The auto company conducted regular surveys of customer satisfaction as indicators or metrics of success. Unfortunately, those surveys did not measure the buying criteria used by their customers. The survey, for example, asked how satisfied the customers were with many facets of the service area. As a result of these surveys, the company learned that customers loved those leather chairs in the waiting room and that their shop floors were clean enough to eat from. But the surveys did not determine what made customers buy their car and, more important, what would make them buy that brand again. The auto company was asking plenty of questions, but it wasn't asking questions that identified and linked to the things that actually influenced buying behavior and loyalty. The company found that its survey was off target when market share plummeted.

For its part, IBM also found out that some of its survey tools were wrong. At about the time the auto company was winning its award, IBM was working to become customer focused and to compete on customer-defined ideal delivery of value. Early in this effort, IBM targeted several customer-facing business processes for improvement. These included the customer order fulfillment and customer billing processes. Each was systematically mapped and documented in great detail. Reengineering approaches were introduced into these processes, along with business process ownership and horizontal, cross-functional process management disciplines. In short, IBM was attempting to do everything by the book, according to the leading thinkers of the time. The problem was that while academics and management gurus of the early to mid-1990s were expounding upon obliterating and reengineering existing ways of doing business, their approaches failed to consider methodically the customers' view. To develop a truly customer-focused vision, new customer research techniques had to be developed.

On initially using these new CVM customer-visioning approaches (described in Chapter 5), IBM management received a surprise. Customers identified specific process performance criteria that actually influence their buying decisions. And on reviewing traditional customer satisfaction surveys, which they had been conducting for years, IBM—much like the auto company—learned that the surveys did not include questions regarding many of those critical customer-defined buying criteria. Customer satisfaction had been tracked all right, but not regarding several of the must-have needs that customers use to determine whether a vendor is meeting their basic expectations, nor were other high-value needs being surveyed that the customers said would differentiate a company's service processes and attract customer share. The firm had measured and religiously tracked a multiyear trendline of customer opinion on topics of great interest to the corporation and had successfully attained key internal performance metrics. But in many cases, the overall target of buyer loyalty and related market share improvement was missed. Managing by internally derived objectives had been distracting management's focus and obscuring the attainment of desired customer goals.

IBM and the auto company sincerely wanted customer input. Both corporations had, for many years, spent a considerable amount of time, money, and effort tracking customer opinions. Those opinions had a significant impact on how the companies ran their business and on investments that were made for improvement. Unfortunately, and typically, many of the questions and methods employed were seriously off target. Again, good managers with good intentions were simply not enough.

Stepping Outside and Looking In

So what is the solution? As IBM learned, an outside-in viewpoint is required to enable a company to be truly customer driven. The old management by objectives paradigm must change from an inside-out model of internally defined goals and objectives to a radically different, outside-in, customer-defined set of objectives (Figure 2-2).

In this example, rather than using an internal view (Where do *we* want to be?), the company secures a highly actionable, customer-defined vision of itself as the ideal provider of products and services. This customer view (Where do our *customers* want us to be?) becomes the focal point for the business strategy and operations. The customers' needs and wants also serve as the key metrics to be probed and tracked in subsequent customer opinion surveys.

Using the customer to help design products is not new (e.g., personal stereo systems, color selection in appliances, etc.); however, using what customers value to engineer business processes and service delivery is a new and emerging discipline. Customer value management provides a systematic, customer-centric means to attain bottom-line goals of growth and profitability.

Managing by Customer Vision: What do our CUSTOMERS want us ideally to be, and what must change to get there?

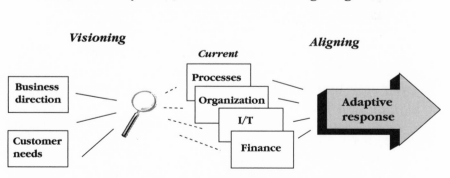

Result = A customer-focused business strategy

Figure 2-2 The new reality: Management 2001 (© Copyright IBM, 1999)

The Factory Floor: Birthplace of Customer- Defined Processes

Like many back office or administrative process improvement approaches, several of the customer-driven approaches outlined in this book have their origins in manufacturing processes. Many academics agree there is often a five-year lag between the introduction of new approaches to improve core manufacturing processes and the appearance of those same methods in the "softer" business processes. As examples, consider process mapping, process analysis techniques, statistical quality control, benchmarking, and reengineering, all of which appeared initially in the areas of manufacturing and production, and all of which years later became staples in the management of other operational business processes.

To understand the next wave of "innovative" business process tools and techniques, one may only need to look at manufacturing to see new approaches that could be coming down the path to administrative processes in five or ten years. For example, when IBM began to innovate and utilize customer-focused outcome-oriented business process reengineering, we developed several techniques similar to the quality function deployment (QFD) approaches Ford Motor Company used to design the Ford Taurus (Figure 2-3), which became one of the best selling cars in America.

In a *Harvard Business Review* article, "House of Quality" (May 1988), Dr. Akao introduced the world to the concepts of QFD. Quality function deployment is a discipline for taking customers' needs, applying a quantitative importance weighting to them, and then working (somewhat like reverse engineering) through a series of matrices to define the specific product attributes that are necessary to meet those customer needs. Finally, by working even further backward, it is possible to derive the actual design specifications of the components and individual parts required to build the product.

Following this principle, Ford Motor Company had the customers in their target marketplace define a vision of the Taurus as a preferred vehicle. Using this customer input, everything from the functions of intermittent windshield wipers to the sound of a door closing became the customer-defined design points for the new vehicle. ("We like to hear a deep *chunk* sound," said several cus-

Quality Function Deployment (QFD)

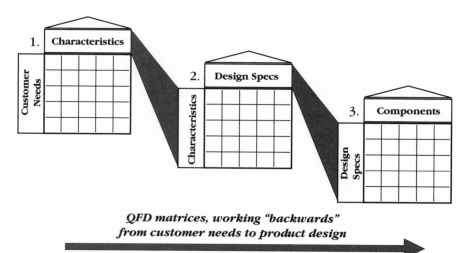

*QFD matrices, working "backwards"
from customer needs to product design*

Figure 2-3 Quality function deployment (QFD): Using the voice of the customer in manufacturing to design and engineer products

tomers.) The results are history, and the Taurus has attained unprecedented market acceptance and success.

We wondered, if back office or administrative process disciplines lag, but follow, successful approaches to improve product development and manufacturing, could a QFD-like approach be utilized to engineer business capabilities to fulfill a customer vision of a company being the preferred service provider?

Dr. John Henderson of Boston University was working with an IBM consultant on an engagement at a retailer's headquarters in Canada. He utilized a framework similar to the conceptual framework of QFD. With Dr. Henderson's approach, a company could begin with desired business outcomes (i.e., attain specific business metrics regarding low cost, market share, etc.) and work backward (inward into the company) to derive the process characteristics and the enabling infrastructure which should also be measured to assure attainment of the desired outcome metric. Professor Henderson intended his framework to be used as a vehicle to establish a comprehensive set of performance metrics for a business enterprise (Figure 2-4).

The Henderson measurement framework captured the dependencies for a business function by establishing first, "What are the

**Aligning Desired Business Outcomes
with the Requisite Process Capabilities and Infrastructure**

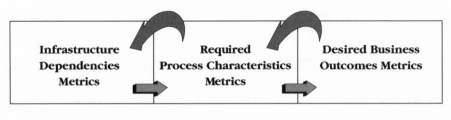

| Infrastructure Dependencies Metrics | Required Process Characteristics Metrics | Desired Business Outcomes Metrics |

**Horizontally linked
measurement system**

Figure 2-4 Henderson three-cell: Linking business outcomes to infrastructure (Adapted from work by Prof. John Henderson)

desired outcomes?" Then the management team was led to identify, "What process characteristics must be working well to attain the desired business outcome?" Moreover, "What measurements should be in place for those processes?" Finally, "What elements of infrastructure must be functioning well to enable the processes? and What measurements should be in place to ensure this?"

Using this technique, the same horizontal logic and linkage could also be depicted, but on a vertical plane, to comprise a more complete view of the relationships between the individual employee (and attaining metrics at the individual level), the department (and how individual employees collectively result in department attainment), and the enterprise (and how departments cumulatively result in attaining the enterprise-level measurements and objectives). As Figure 2-5 depicts, the result is a nine-cell framework for an integrated measurement system, depicting horizontally what to measure as in-process metrics to attain the desired final outcomes and vertically what to measure as individual or department metrics to attain enterprise results. At the end of the session, the retailer's CFO exclaimed, "You have captured my company on a single page!"

Professor Henderson's nine-cell framework demonstrated both the horizontal and the vertical alignment and linkages that must be in place to attain business success. By identifying these relationships, the framework allowed specific metrics or measurements to be put into place to ensure that the components of each cell were functioning as required in support of the others.

Horizontally and Vertically Linked
Measurement System

	Infrastructure Metrics	Process Characteristics Metrics	Business Outcome Metrics
Individual	Individual Employee Infrastructure Metrics	Individual-Level, In-Process Performance Metrics	Individual Employee OUTCOMES Metrics
Department	Department-Level Infrastructure Metrics	Department-Level, In-Process Performance Metrics	Department OUTCOMES Metrics
Enterprise	Enterprise-Level Infrastructure Metrics	Enterprise-Level In-process Metrics	Enterprise OUTCOMES Metrics

Figure 2-5 Henderson nine-cell: Linking business outcomes to infrastructure at employee, department, and enterprise levels (Adapted from work by Prof. John Henderson)

In reflecting on Dr. Henderson's work, the IBM consultant had a breakthrough reaction, "One could combine this concept with that of QFD," he thought, "and actually design a customer-envisioned process or a company starting with customer-defined needs and wants at the far right of the matrix and working inward (right to left) to derive the required process capabilities and then further inward to identify the specific infrastructure enablers required" (Figure 2-6).

At that point, CVM was born!

Customer value management is a logical framework that aligns and links a firm's infrastructure with the process capabilities necessary to attain customer-defined, measurable outcomes. Infrastructure is viewed simply as a supporting foundation on which business process abilities are enabled. The capabilities, in turn, must be measured, aligned, and linked with the customer-envisioned outcomes that will influence buyer behavior to attract and grow market share.

The remainder of this book is devoted to the issues, approaches, pitfalls, and competitive benefits that companies will experience when using such a formal, systematic approach to compete and grow based on delivering customer value. Customer value management begins with identifying the top of the pyramid (see Figure 2-7) and determining your current and future customers' vision of an ideal you.

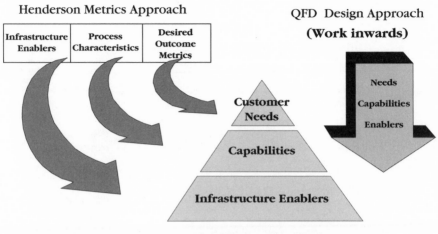

CVM Framework

Figure 2-6 Combining concepts: Using a QFD-like approach, starting with customer-desired outcomes, to envision an aligned set of business capabilities and infrastructure (© Copyright IBM, 1999)

Figure 2-7 The journey begins: Developing a customer-envisioned, ideal business (© Copyright IBM, 1999)

In Chapter 3 we address the critical issue of determining whose view counts in your customer-defined vision, which surprisingly is one of the more difficult tasks in becoming customer focused.

EXERCISE
Applying CVM to Your Business

Management Issues

How do you create and then fulfill a customer-defined vision of your company as their preferred provider? How do you move from internally focused management by objectives to customer-centered metrics and business design?

1. Managing by (customer-defined) objectives
   - What are your business measurements and objectives regarding customers?
   - Who defined them? Are they an internal view of what customers want? Or are they an outside-in customer-defined view?
   - How might you secure a more actionable outside-in view?
   - What is your customers' outside-in vision of an ideal you?
   - How is this view compatible with, reflected in, and linked to your other business goals, objectives, and strategies?
   - How are customer opinion and satisfaction survey questions linked to what actually drives the buying behavior of your customers?

2. Engineering business capabilities by (customer-vision) desired outcomes
   - Do you have only business or process outcome (historical results) measures? Or do you also have in-process measures that alert you just in time to issues with prerequisite process capabilities or infrastructure?
   - Can you use that knowledge to pinpoint business process and infrastructure design weaknesses and to engineer improvements?

3

Focus

The Top of the CVM Pyramid: Whose View Counts?

The first step in marksmanship...
is to select the target!
ROBIN OF LOCKSLEY

Not everyone is a current or future desirable, high-value customer whose opinions and viewpoint should drive business design and investments. Therefore, identifying and focusing on a targeted set of customers whose view counts become the critical first step to develop and implement a customer-defined business vision for products and services.

Throughout its history, IBM has been renowned for its rigorous training program for newly hired marketing representatives. One thing that was intentionally or unintentionally driven into many a new employee's mind in IBM's earlier days was that selling large mainframe computers was the route to their financial success. An oft-told story was of an enterprising young man who took this news in stride. With tongue planted firmly in his cheek, he quipped, "I'll just sell typewriters; after all, the commission on typewriters for 30,000 customers should be about equal to one mainframe computer!"

This new sales representative may have identified a way to attain his objectives, but his route to success, if taken seriously, wasn't going to be easy. He had targeted and would have had to meet personally the needs of thousands of low-revenue customers.

Considering the high-cost sales techniques that were common during that earlier era, it was probably not a good idea. Today, however, by engineering cost-efficient processes to meet the needs of high-volume, low-margin customers, companies and their employees can enjoy great success and profitability (more on that later). That young salesperson's quandary, however, continues to be one of the single most important issues and critical factors in business: the selection and targeting of an appropriate, desired set of customers.

Although this may sound like an elementary and fairly simple activity, it is not.

IBM: Becoming Customer Focused. When IBM began transforming from a centralized, internally focused culture to a decentralized, customer-focused organization, management recognized the need for a strong top-down message to kickoff the initiative. This message would signal to employees that this was more than a passing marketing campaign. Every person in the company, worldwide, was challenged to identify their customers and develop a plan for meeting those customers' needs.

I was a midlevel manager at that time and was scheduled to travel to an off-site meeting just as we were asked to develop the plan. While away, I wanted my staff to begin to identify their customers and determine how to service them. My organization was a headquarters support function that provided services to other IBM entities (internal customers). I assembled my team of managers, reviewed the corporate directive, and asked them to meet with their employees on the following day. "While I am gone," I said, "you and your staff must do one simple thing—decide who your customers are. On my return, we will go to your customers and discuss their needs and how we can provide them."

I then boarded an airplane and flew to New York. On arriving at my hotel, there was an urgent message to call a junior manager at my office. He was quite upset when I finally reached him. "Get back here as soon as you can," said an agitated voice on the telephone. "A major argument broke out in our meeting regarding who is our customer!" Feelings were so intense that the young manager had quickly ended the meeting. Amazingly, this was from a department comprised of veteran employees who had been working side-by-side for many years.

Employees who had been coworkers and performed the same job for years could not agree on the ultimate recipient of value for the services they performed. Moreover, their individual opinions regarding the identity of their customers were not only diverse, but also passionately held. The manager who had called me said, "At that moment, I realized that this market-driven, customer-focus thing was going to be much more difficult than I had ever imagined!"

Who Is the Actual Customer? Approver? Buyer? User? Channel? Staff and Influencers?

As the IBM story illustrates, not everyone is going to agree on the identity of the customer. However, when developing, implementing, and maintaining a customer-defined business vision, that fundamental issue must be resolved by asking, "Who is our actual customer? Who receives the value from our products and services, which in turn creates the demand and therefore a market for them? When we develop our outside-in, customer-defined vision, whose view counts?"

The needs from groups or segments of highly desired customers should collectively become the key design points for business improvement and engineering. But where in the value chain of customer relationships (Figure 3-1) do we place the pointer to identify those people?

- At the point of purchase (where the contracts person or buyer is the customer).

- At the point of purchase approval (where the financial reviewer or provider of funding is the customer).

- At the point of product or service provision (where the channel or third-party value-adder is the customer).

- At the point of product or service receipt (where the shipping and receiving staff is the customer).

- At the point of product or service consumption (where the end user or consumer is the customer).

Next...Who Is the Customer? Whose Opinion Counts?

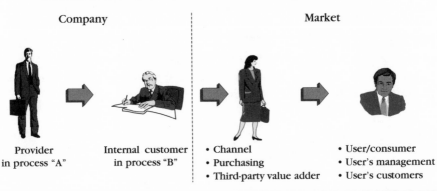

Company   Market

| Provider in process "A" | Internal customer in process "B" | • Channel
• Purchasing
• Third-party value adder | • User/consumer
• User's management
• User's customers |

Supplier/Customer Value Chain

Figure 3-1 Identifying the customer: Analyzing the value chain to see whose view counts (© Copyright IBM, 1999)

- Or even beyond the point of consumption (where a downstream recipient of value or benefit from the end user is potentially an ultimate customer).

Figure 3-1 depicts a series of supplier and customer relationships that cumulatively result in the delivery of a product or service to an ultimate end customer. Each of the parties depicted is a potential customer whose view is important.

- A customer/consumer may be the person or organization that is at the point of interaction with the product, service, or process and possibly the ultimate end user.

- A customer/channel may be a person or organization that buys or handles the product or service, often as an intermediary for other users.

- An internal customer or process is part of the company's value-add chain of processes that provide products or services to the external customers.

Each of the foregoing may have a combined "supplier/customer" role within the overall value chain that delivers the product or service to the ultimate using customer. Identifying and securing the viewpoints of each may be important, depending on the scope of the business issue under study (e.g., an internal process, an external customer-facing process, or multicompany cross-enterprise processes).

1. The Customer View at the Point-of-Contact Interaction

Who is at the direct point of interaction with your company's products, services, and processes? The person who resides at a specific point of interaction is a customer of that process who can potentially receive benefit or value at that moment. Those individuals can also be disappointed and experience dissatisfaction. Understanding the needs of individuals who interact directly with company processes and services provides a valuable starting point for customer visioning and subsequent business improvement. A key question is: How much impact do these parties have on the buying decision and what importance will they play in overall "paying-customer" loyalty and repeat buying behavior? For example, travel agents and secretaries are not the paying customer or the approver of expenditures or the end user/consumer of airline reservations and tickets. Does their view count? To determine whether travel agents' opinions should be pursued as a design point for the business vision, one must consider their influence on the buying behavior of those who are true end users, consumers, and purchasers.

To become a premier provider of air transportation to the flying public, an airline must satisfy many constituents other than the most obvious consumers of the product, the travelers. It would be important to start at the point of direct interaction and work outward to identify all possible additional players on the customer side of the relationship. Using that perspective, travel agents are integral players in the overall value chain between the seller (airlines) and the consumer (private individuals and business travelers). Further, they are powerful influencers of the ultimate buying decision by either directly representing consumers in the transactions or by advising them on which of several alternatives to select.

Additional examples of nonend users or nonconsumers who receive value from your processes at the point of contact include:

- Customer purchasing and contracts staff as they interact with your company's sales and order processes or customer service.
- Customer shipping and receiving staff as they interact with your company's delivery processes.
- Customer accounts payable personnel as they interact with your billing, invoicing, and accounts receivable processes.

In these examples, the party at the point of contact with your company's products, services, or processes could be either a private individual or someone from a commercial entity (i.e., a consumer or a corporation). Commercial corporate customers offer the more complex scenarios for identifying whose view counts, particularly when considering their array of both direct contact and nondirect contact customers. The people who interface directly with your company (although many may not be direct users and consumers of your products or services) are very important. The extent to which your processes or service interactions add cost or complexity to these parties is an opportunity to develop a vision from their viewpoint that could make your company a preferred provider.

2. The Customer View from Non-Point-of-Contact Personnel and Influencers

When looking at the value chain between the company and the paying customer, an indirect chain of events must also be considered: the non-point-of-contact activities that lead to a buying decision (review of alternatives, selection, approval, and funding). Again, parties who may not actually use the product, process, or service may have a significant influence on its selection or reuse. It is critical to understand the paying customer's processes for decision making so that the top portion of our customer vision pyramid includes not only the viewpoints of point-of-contact personnel and users/consumers, but also that of the parties who make the buying decision and their advisers. Others whose views count in a customer vision include nondirect-contact influencers of customer opinion such as reviewers, approvers, staff expert advisers, consultants, and sources of information or counsel regarding alternative products and services.

Comerica Bank: Identifying the Non-Point-of-Contact Influencers. When Comerica Bank conducted a CVM study to understand the needs and wants of a targeted market segment in order to attract them, the customers were also asked: Whom do you turn to for information regarding your alternatives for financial products and services?

The small-business customers responded that many sources outside of their direct interactions with the bank affect their buying decisions, including:

- Manufacturers suggest alternative financing sources to purchase their products.
- Services vendors often provide financing recommendations.
- Publications and journalists advise small businesses on financing.
- Software on the market can provide financial planning tools and databases of alternative sources.
- Accountants provide advice on potential sources of funds, lease versus buy decisions, and fixed versus variable rates.

However, the banking customers also identified circumstances under which the bank itself would be their preferred source of information regarding sources of financing. For example, they said that if there is an existing relationship with the small business, then the bank loan officers could be a primary source for advice on financing alternatives.

Armed with this information, Comerica could then take two important actions:

1. Give customers what they want: Engineer capabilities and infrastructure to ensure that a relationship exists for every key customer, positioning the bank as the preferred provider of information and counsel.
2. Influence the influencers: Engineer capabilities and infrastructure to regularly secure the needs, wants, and values of the other sources of customer information and include their viewpoint in

the vision for the new company products, processes, and services because their view counts.

The bank's customers could just as easily have said that a wide array of customer internal experts, financial staff, and management participate in, review, or approve their buying decisions. All of these parties must be identified, their leverage determined regarding buyer behavior, loyalty, and repeat business, and a decision made regarding incorporating their views, needs, and values into the company product, process, or service vision.

IBM Order Fulfillment: Using Point-of-Contact, Decision-Maker, and Influencer Viewpoints. When IBM began work to reengineer its order fulfillment processes using a CVM customer-defined vision of an ideal vendor, the first questions to be resolved were: Who are the customers of this process? Whose view counts?

The subsequent research to secure an outside-in vision for reengineering was far ranging and provided a broad customer-view perspective. First, the needs of the individual geographies were compared by holding focus groups in several diverse locations (U.S. sessions were conducted in New York City; Paramus, NJ; Chicago, IL; Atlanta, GA; St. Louis, MO; and Los Angeles, CA). Next, differences in commercial customers' needs were probed by securing research participants from multiple industries (automotive, distribution, retail, banking and financial services, manufacturing, process, healthcare, transportation, telecommunications, etc.). Differences in needs based on customer size were examined by including very small, mid-size, large, megacorporations, and global corporations. Then the different needs or viewpoints of point-of-contact personnel versus noncontact influencers within these companies were gathered by recruiting participants from purchasing, shipping and receiving, accounts payable, information technology (I/T) operations, legal, finance, and other corporate functions.

Within these groups, IBM obtained a balanced view from both executives of the organizations (decision makers) and their support staff (influencers of decision makers). Finally, IBM recruited both its own customers and the customers of key competitors for the focus groups. At the end of the visioning stage, critical findings were developed regarding the common or different needs of these groups and, importantly, the level of common versus unique IBM infrastructure required to satisfy them. IBM later confirmed and prioritized these findings during more widely based quantitative surveys. (See Chapter 6, Prioritization: Making Investment Decisions Based on Buying Behavior.)

3. The Customer View from the Channel or Third-Party Value Chain Intermediaries

Another customer whose view must be considered is the channel. Channels are vehicles or intermediaries for delivering products or services, and they may be internal (e.g., a telephone call center) or external (e.g., agents, dealerships, retail outlets). A major topic of discussion between consultants and their clients is often focused on the treatment of channels as customers. A common view among both manufacturers (e.g., automobile companies) and providers of "soft" products and services (e.g., insurance and financial services) is that the primary customers to be satisfied are their channels: dealers, distributors, franchisees, insurance agents, financial advisers, and just about anybody who deals with the ultimate end user. Virtually any company dealing with channels would dearly like to treat the end consumer as their customer. However, these companies are highly dependent on third-party channels or intermediaries, who often have a proprietary view of owning the consumer relationship. In this situation, the channel occupies a position of power by being a control point in the value chain, interfacing directly with the end customer, and often with the leverage to direct customer purchases to multiple providers. While the product or service manufacturer may own the brand and suffer the deterioration of its image due to poor channel performance, the channel owns the actual customer relationship.

Most CEOs would like to avoid an either–or scenario (either service the channel or the customer). They would profit greatly by a means to effectively recognize the channel as an important customer or stakeholder in the value chain and also to ensure the delivery of what the end customer needs and values. In other words, they want to be able to go beyond the proposition that either the channel or the consumer is their customer. This problem becomes even more pronounced with the emergence of the

Internet, which provides greater ease of direct contact between the consumer and manufacturer. Manufacturers must nourish both a direct consumer relationship as well as their more traditional channel-as-customer relationships.

A CVM approach to business engineering facilitates both relationships. The best way to become the ideal provider to a channel is to find out what its customers want and then design the company processes to enable the channel to be ideal to the end customer. With this approach, a company may gain the best of both worlds. By satisfying both constituencies (channel and consumer), the channel's objections are removed regarding the company becoming too intimate with the end customer. An investment by the company to understand consumer-defined value and associated behavior drivers becomes a value-add to the channel.

Harley-Davidson Motorcycles: Using the Channel and Customer Viewpoints.

Harley-Davidson has been a success story of the 1990s, going from the edge of bankruptcy to high customer retention and cult-like loyalty. A decade earlier, Harley-Davidson motorcycles (other than the vintage restored models) sat ignored in showrooms and often with cardboard from the shipping crates underneath to protect the showroom floor from oil dripping from new models. Today, Harley-Davidson dealerships have order backlogs that are several months long, and the company strategy calls for increasing plants and capacity by over 200 percent by the year 2003 (the one-hundredth anniversary of the brand). How did Harley-Davidson achieve such a turnaround? They did several things that collectively reengineered the manufacturing and other core processes of the company and focused relentlessly on the needs of the customer.

And whom does Harley-Davidson define as their customer? The answer is: They do not have one customer set; they have two! Understanding whose view counts, Harley-Davidson has their products, processes, services, satisfaction metrics, and employee team incentives linked and aligned with two sets of customers: the motorcyclists and the dealerships.

Central to Harley-Davidson's measurements and metrics of success are two parallel customer satisfaction indices: a customer satisfaction index (CSI) and a dealer satisfaction index (DSI). By focusing on both, Harley-Davidson has attained a balanced delivery of value by going directly to the paying consumer, while maintaining trust and credibility with its channel of dealerships.

Last year, at the company's annual motorcycle rally at Sturgess, SD, over 500,000 enthusiasts showed up. That's a powerful statement to the loyalty customers feel toward the brand. Today, the brand has developed such a fierce loyalty and value that used Harley-Davidson bikes often sell for much more than new ones. Additionally, dealer satisfaction and enthusiasm closely mirror that of their end customers.

Our conclusion is that treating dealers as a customer and using a CVM approach to understand dealers' needs, wants, and values are a good way to manage and maintain channel loyalty. However, also including the end customers of your channel in the CVM analysis and engineering the company capabilities to ideally enable the channel to meet its end customers' needs can be far more powerful.

4. The Customer View from Internal Customers

A major point of contention in many companies—as they move toward horizontal business process management and become customer focused—is the issue of whether or not there are two customers for internal processes. One is an internal "little c" customer, and the other is the "big C" external paying Customer. Again, the challenge here is determining whose view should count. The legitimacy of internal customers has been cause for endless heated debates, with parties on both sides of the issue taking strongly held positions. Just recall my experience a few years ago within IBM!

Advocates who feel big C is the only legitimate customer maintain that there can be only one customer—the paying customer. In many cases, this position is rooted in prior experiences where internal customers have made exorbitant demands on internal suppliers that seemed baseless. For example, although IBM was an early pioneer of business process management, the company lost potential benefits due to an initial focus on meeting the needs of internal customers. IBM's original approach to improve the cross-functional flow of work (process management) focused heavily on obtaining an interlock between the internal customer–supplier relationships that comprise a business process. Further, the internal customers often set arbitrary objectives such as one-hour turnaround or 50 percent cost reduction on their internal suppliers. The problem was that the internal customers were each viewed as a stand-alone customer entity rather than in the context of their position in a value chain to the external customer.

When we initiated CVM, our process management pioneers changed their focus to the external big C Customer. They positioned the internal customer–supplier relationships into the context of a value chain, and positive things began to happen:

- The big C Customer became the design point (whose view counted most) for process engineering, management, and improvement.

- The internal customers each had to rationalize their requirements to their internal suppliers by showing how they cumulatively (end to end) linked to meet the ultimate big C Customer needs and wants.

- Internal silos and resistance to change were broken down by using the voice of the paying customer as the final arbiter for decisions and priority setting.

- Internal metrics and measures were aligned with (and resulted in the attainment of) external customers metrics of success.

- The subsequent improvement and attainment of internal metric performance resulted in dramatic improvements in external customer (market) value and business success.

Our findings and conclusions regarding internal versus external customers are that the scope of most business processes or customer issues being addressed should be linked to an impact on a paying external customer in order to anchor to a desired external business result (see Chapter 4, Scope: Selecting Highest Leverage Customer Interactions). This linkage positions the subsequent analysis to make the big C (or paying customer's) view the final arbiter and design point for business improvement actions. In this context, the internal customer–supplier value chain relationships are also legitimate and must be included in the business process visioning and subsequent design of business capabilities and infrastructure.

Targeting the Right Customer

Why Not All Customers?

Once the potential customer contact points and influencers are identified, another fundamental issue must be resolved: Which customers are actually desired? In other words, all customers are not equal in current or future potential value, so which of these should you target and make investments to attract?

The marketplace can be segmented in many different ways to enable you to avoid spreading your resources indiscriminately and trying to be all things to all customers. Customers and prospective customers may be rationally grouped into market segments, each with its own potential for profitability. For example, Dell Computer may target its direct-sales effort primarily at corporate customers, as opposed to MicroCenter trying to sell PCs to everyone. Trade magazines are particularly good at segmenting audiences with specific interests (hobbies, professions, sports, etc.).

In our experience, customer and market segmentation is one of the most powerful, overlooked, and underutilized tools of management today. As a result, it is common for major corporations to expend huge sums across a broad array of customers and prospects with little or no regard for their relative current (or future) profitability or for their individual needs, wants, or buying behaviors. The firms that do utilize one or more of these dimensions to drive focused, targeted marketing actions will typically fail to use the same disciplines to engineer their business capabilities and have their processes and services become equally segment focused. Either way, for targeted marketing or for business engineering, segmentation allows a company to select and then focus on a specific targeted set of customers or prospects.

Focus on Segments and "Segments of One"

The battle to attract and retain loyal customers, given today's technology, will be fought and won based on the ability to identify potentially profitable current and future market segments and then meet their specific needs. Of course, effective segmentation of a marketplace must go beyond analyzing the current customers of a firm. It must include the ability to identify and then appeal to non-customers who are members (or potential members) of desirable market segments. This has become less of a challenge, especially for companies that are harvesting their own customer data by using sophisticated data warehouse and data mining technologies. By merging customer data with noncustomer market data acquired from outside sources, these firms can group prospects into mirror images, or "resemblers," of their known profitable customer base. In effect, it puts names and faces onto the external target market, allowing the company to do micromarketing by aligning noncustomers with groups of profitable customers.

Unfortunately, most companies today (particularly those with the largest volume of transactions) are unable to determine and track profit at the individual customer level. The typical bank or financial services institution, for example, does not know which customers are highly profitable and which are not. If they did know, then high-value customers and prospects could be further divided into subsegments with similar needs and wants. These highly profitable, needs-based microsegments could then be appealed to via targeted marketing and by engineering segment-focused business processes and services to meet their needs. In this manner, broad groups of individuals with similar profitability and sharing common needs could be attracted and retained en masse as profit-based market segments.

However, pressures are building for firms to move even beyond such a focus on the needs of segments. In today's environment, it is becoming increasingly common for customers to expect tailored, personalized treatment. Collectively, a segment of like-minded customers (or prospective customers) may represent a significant revenue opportunity, but with some very rare exceptions (e.g., personal banking for the super rich), personalized treatment would be inefficient and unprofitable. For the lower value customers in particular, the quandary is one of low marginal profitability to the company per individual transaction versus a customer's need to receive highly personalized treatment. Such a segment can actually be profitable, however, if a means can be found to meet the needs of the individ-

uals within the group efficiently. Here is where technology and segmentation can jointly play a role. By mining your company's customer transaction data to identify groupings of customers with
similar buying behaviors, it becomes possible to use the CVM
approach to attract that segment, the hypothesis being that they
behave similarly because they have similar underlying needs.
Grouping individuals with similar needs makes it possible for your
company to develop deliverables that meet the needs of the group,
but often with the appearance of personalized delivery, by using
cost-efficient mass-production processes.

For example, clustering targeted customers by common needs
provides you with design points to develop processes with several
sets of (modularized) capabilities rather than being "one size fits all."
The different process modules, each with a single efficient deliverable, collectively enable you to do things in many different ways. In
effect, each process "capability module" is designed to attain the efficiencies of mass production while providing only one process or
service deliverable alternative out of several customer-preferred
ways. Examples might include having the ability to provide a customer's billing on a single invoice or on separate invoices by product type or by customer-user department. By capturing how each
member of a segment wants to be treated and accessing the data
later at the point of service delivery (i.e., at order, billing, postsale
service, etc.), the appropriate service process capability module may
be "snapped in," just in time, for the appearance of personalized, tailored service (my invoice, my way). From the company's perspective, however, the normal efficiencies of standardized, efficient, and
effective business processes are being enjoyed, which is the benefit
of having engineered new mass-customization business capabilities.

Today, most firms categorize their customers into groupings based
on the types and volume of products they consume, not on their
margin of profit or on the basis of common needs and wants. Those
companies could be learning more about their customers and by
using that knowledge, drive increased growth and profit. Current
technology allows a firm to create sophisticated data warehouses
that can mine millions of transactions to better understand customers
at an individual level, group them into profit- and needs-based
microsegments, and access that information for (the appearance of)
personalized service delivery.

Comerica Bank 2: Finding Out Whose View Counts in Your Own Data Files.
Comerica Bank, located in the midwestern United States and
faced with the issue of how to optimize and leverage the relationships and potential of its small-business segment, turned to its
own customer information. The bank collected data from across
the enterprise, literally wrung from silo to silo, as millions of
transactions were accumulated which had previously been
unconnected and not correlated. Tens of thousands of small businesses were separated into groupings of companies with similar
buying behaviors and transaction volumes. The combinations of
products and services consumed, coupled with volumes and sea-
sonal fluctuations, were analyzed by algorithms, which found
patterns of similarity that would otherwise be unnoticeable. This
provided groupings of firms in which some unknown common
interests and values were resulting in common behavior, such as
the types of products or services consumed and the timing and
trends of financial transactions.

The bank then probed some specific groupings that appeared to
have the potential for high future value. For example, there was a
group which had virtually all the characteristics of another group
except that one had highly profitable loans with the bank and the
other group had no loans. This information alone was extremely
valuable in enabling targeted marketing to the group without loans,
as they apparently shared characteristics and behaviors with another highly desired segment. Further, by identifying resemblers in the
marketplace who were not current bank customers but who mir-
rored or resembled these profitable customers (or users of a particular product), the bank could also efficiently market to a potentially
high-profit set of prospects.

However, by introducing the CVM approach, the bank was able
to leverage these data further. A vision of ideal value from bank
loan products, services, and processes emerged by conducting
focus group visioning sessions with members of both segments. By
developing this vision and securing an assessment of current bank
performance against the vision from customers, the bank is now in
a position to go far beyond mere targeted marketing. Such an
approach can literally drive customer-vision-based engineering of
the bank's actual business capabilities, focused on a high-profit
market segment.

Consider the Cost (and Return on Investment) of Meeting Their Needs

Ultimately, segment selection and targeting must rest on the cost and return associated with building and maintaining the actual business capabilities to deliver a segment's envisioned value. In some cases, segments are self-selecting. This occurs when a company's existing capabilities are found to align easily with the needs of a segment or when emerging technologies enable the profitable creation of new capabilities that will appeal to specific segments. In other cases, a reconciliation of segment needs versus current business processes, products, and services will reveal that the financial investment needed to attain the required capability level is not practical. Segments become a portfolio of alternatives to be analyzed as business opportunities, each with a different cost–return ratio.

Portfolios of segments must be managed, meaning that some must be discarded (firing the customer) rather than simply engaging in a one-way game of acquiring segments, or only drawing new segment cards to increase your hand. CVM can help identify which segments must become the discards due to the lack of compatibility between segments' needs and affordable business capabilities.

An important concept in CVM is that it is a two-way street: Customer value must be considered in light of both the value received from a customer (return) and the value provided to a customer (cost). There must be a rational and profitable balance between the two (Figure 3-2).

Companies are becoming increasingly concerned with being all things to all customers, without regard to how profitable a customer is. Figure 3-2 depicts an environment that is common to most major companies. They are unable to:

- Determine the relative value from or profitability of different customers.

- Vary the level of service value provided to (and costs of) different customers.

For companies that are able to identify their high- versus low-value customers, an alternative to providing homogeneous high-cost services to customers who are of relatively low value to the company is

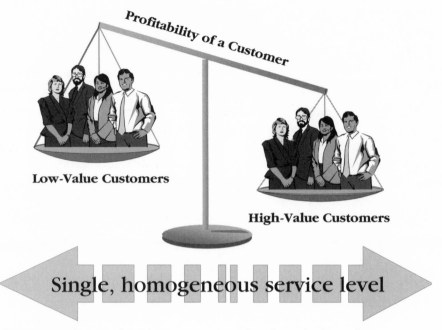

Figure 3-2 Balancing the value proposition: What about the low-value customers? (© Copyright IBM, 1999)

to deselect that segment. The firm can overtly decide not to recruit new members of this segment and/or end the unprofitable business relationship with existing members. However, there are alternatives to spreading high-cost services and processes indiscriminately across all customers or firing low-value customers. An option to being all things to all customers is to provide different things to different customers based on their value to you. The concepts of segmentation and "not all customers or prospects" still apply. However, the application becomes "not the same value to all customers and prospects at the same price" (Figure 3-3).

In Figure 3-3, balance is attained by providing a consistent level of service to everyone via a single set of common support infrastructure and capabilities, but varying the fees for that service. The low-profit customers are charged more for the service. Higher value customers are charged lower fees, thereby providing them with greater value commensurate with their contribution to the company.

A different approach is to exploit the value of high-leverage processes and services by rewarding only the most desirable cus-

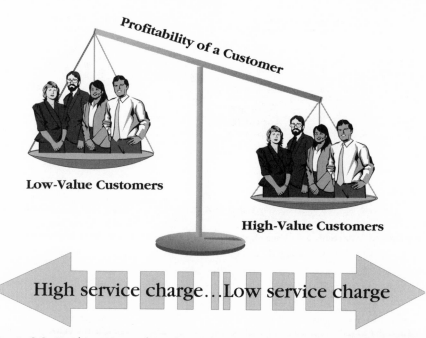

Figure 3-3 An alternative to firing low-value customers: Charge a fee for services to recover your costs (© Copyright IBM, 1999)

tomers with extraordinary service. In this scenario, firms may choose to differentiate themselves by varying the service levels and providing customer-defined high-value services only to their high-value customers (Figure 3-4).

By pinpointing customers' relative profitability (current and future), companies may vary the level of service and attain a balance between value received from and value provided to customers. In Figure 3-4, the company vision results in business capabilities which provide low-value customers with only their basic must-have needs, while providing higher value customers with additional higher value services that attract, delight, and retain them. Airline frequent flyer Bronze, Silver, and Gold Level Services provide an excellent example: Travelers are segmented based on their value to the business and then provided with a commensurate level of service.

And yet another strategy is to target both high- and low-value customer segments in the business vision and then engineer capabilities to deliver both tiered services and pricing. The different levels of (tiered) service may each have several (tiered) pricing levels that are

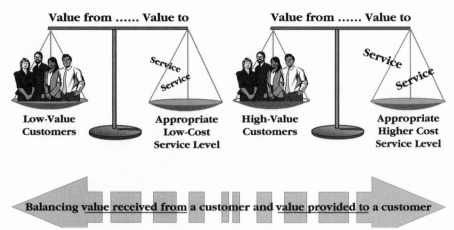

Figure 3-4 Alternative 2: Vary the service levels based on the value of the customer (© Copyright IBM, 1999)

Low-value customers,
who elect to use
higher priced services,
will tend to migrate to higher value.

High-value customers,
who receive higher value
services at lower prices,
will be attracted and retained.

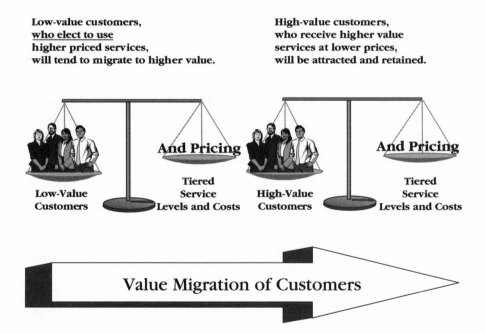

Figure 3-5 An ideal model: Vary both service delivery and pricing to attain balance and migrate customers to higher value (© Copyright IBM, 1999)

charged based on the relative value of the customer receiving them (Figure 3-5).

Low-value customers, in this scenario, must pay an additional fee for extra-value services to attain a balance between value received from a customer and value provided to a customer (Figure 3-5). A variation of this theme is demonstrated by airline lounges that are free to some of the highest valued customers, yet available to lower value and lower profit customers for a fee.

In summary, the selection of whose view counts is not necessarily dependent on who are currently the high-value and high-profit customers. By utilizing the approaches depicted in Figures 3-3 through 3-5, it may be very appropriate to select segments currently considered to be of low value to the company and engineer high-profit capabilities.

How Large Is a Customer Segment? More and More Are Segments of One

Finally, the issue of the size of a target market segment has become a major variable and design point for business strategy. What is the ideal number or size of segments? What about current literature and excitement around the topic of individual segments of one? Should our company be gearing up to deliver products and services to the needs of individuals instead of to major segments?

To answer these questions, one must look at the two primary reasons a firm should perform market segmentation:

1. To identify and target highly desirable customers and potential customers who are of current or future worth to the business.

2. To focus investments in infrastructure, products, services, and process capabilities to provide delivery of value to those segments, be attractive to them, and retain them as customers.

The size of the segments will depend on their natural distribution into groups with similar profitability and common needs, wants, and behaviors. Today, the needs and wants of desirable customers often include their receiving very tailored and personalized products and services. These customers wish to be treated as valued individuals (segments of one) rather than as members of a collective segment. This is becoming a reality across most industries as customers' expectations to receive such treatment are being raised and reinforced daily by highly personalized products and services. However, the concepts outlined in this book are often iterative. For example, it may be only at the later stages of CVM, during the development of the customer-defined vision for targeted segments, that you learn the vision includes meeting some very personalized, individualized needs. It may be then that you discover (or validate your hypothesis) that portions of your segmentation and reengineering may require designing business capabilities to delight segments of one.

There is good news and bad news regarding segments of one. The good news is that emerging technologies are enabling dramatic increases in businesses' ability to get to know customers and to develop and efficiently manufacture, market, and deliver products and services to segments of one. The bad news is that this is an escalating spiral. As technology enables an industry to personalize product and service delivery at a profitable margin, customer expectations quickly rise to make this level of performance an expectation rather than an option. Worse yet, their expectations spill over into nonparallel industries, raising the field of play and the ante to be a player. If your industry does not offer and deliver personalized, tailored products and services today, it most likely will in the very near future. This phenomenon is accelerating at a dramatic pace. And as discussed earlier, what delights the customers of Hertz Corporation also quickly becomes their expectation for Marriott Hotels and Barclays Banks.

For this chapter on segmentation and for purposes of market targeting, the customer may be a sizable segment, or an individual who belongs to a segment of one. The answer will ultimately be determined by examining the scope of customer interactions to be improved (e.g., a specific process or service) and then having the target customers develop their vision of how they wish to be treated.

This brings up our next topic and question to be resolved: Once the customer whose view counts has been defined and targeted, what is the optimum scope of focus for the subsequent vision, analysis, business improvement, and redesign? To answer that question, we turn to Chapter 4.

EXERCISE
Applying CVM to Your Business

Management Issues

To develop a customer view for your particular business, whose view counts?

1. Customer segmentation
   - Who are your desired, targeted customers or market segments?
   - Which of your customers or segments are the high-profit contributors that you wish to grow and that warrant investing in the high-cost service levels that would attract them?
   - Which low-value customers do you wish to retain by understanding and then profitably providing their basic minimum needs?
   - Which low-value customers or segments are potentially future high-profit?
   - How do you identify noncustomers who are potentially high-profit?
   - What are the groupings of customers that have common needs and wants?

2. Customer-vision participants
   - Whose view counts? What criteria determine whom you listen to?
   - Who participates in or influences your target segments' buying decisions?
   - Who is at the direct point-of-contact interaction with your processes?
   - Who receives or could receive value from your processes or services?
   - Who is not in direct interaction but is in the value chain to your customers?
   - Whose opinions will determine whether you grow or decline?

4

Scope

Selecting Highest-Leverage
Customer Interactions

"Change your course by 15°.
I am an admiral."
Came the reply over the radio,
"You change your course by 15°;
I'm a lighthouse!"
                    OLD BUSINESS MEETING JOKE

Understanding your field of play is critical: It defines the competitive battleground and sets a proper scope for business improvement actions. Without such an understanding, the directions and investments made by the management team may be off course or unfocused. Often, the internal view from the bridge of the corporate ship cannot recognize the critical shoals and lighthouses of the marketplace. The ideal way to set the correct improvement scope and course, not surprisingly, is to take the customer view.

An old movie story line tells of a big and impersonal company that decides to expand by buying a smaller company. In this scenario, many of the employees of the smaller company are anxious about the takeover by a giant enterprise, and they begin to resign and take their customers with them. In the confusion, the smaller company's remaining customer base, seeing their favorite business partners gone, also defects. The big conglomerate is left without an expanded business and is financially poorer due to the failed acquisition.

Commercial Bank X.   Life can sometimes imitate art, as was the case with a commercial bank that was rapidly growing via acquisitions and found itself experiencing some severe growth pains.

Although there had not been mass employee resignations, the bank's growth strategy had led to a breakdown in its internal capabilities to provide support and services to its new expanded customer base. Basic processes and services were failing: information on accounts was sometimes wrong; it was taking too long to respond to customer complaints; and accounts from acquired banks were being merged into the new bank's system too slowly, to name a few. As a result, the employees' postmerger anxiety level was rapidly rising, which tended to be passed on to the customers along with the defects. Customer dissatisfaction was becoming a serious issue, particularly on the part of customers from newly acquired banks, who had been receiving outstanding service from their old bank. These customers began to express their discontent in the loudest possible way: They left the bank.

Senior management at the bank knew that changes had to be made—and quickly. They did not want to make the situation worse by implementing wholesale upheavals in how customers did business with the bank. But they knew they must start somewhere; doing nothing was simply not an option. They settled on CVM to analyze the situation and make recommendations, but not for the entire bank. Being conservative, the bank decided to pick a single process scope that would allow the bank to learn CVM and process management. If the new approaches we recommended and implemented did not work, their reasoning went, they would not have many changes to undo.

In light of that thinking, a senior bank executive stated, "We will start with the account analysis process [the business process that ultimately provides a bank statement to commercial customers] because it is not a critical process, and if we 'mess it up,' it will have minimal impact. If that goes well, then we can progress on to the more important higher leverage processes."

So, utilizing CVM, they began their journey to become customer focused by developing a customer-defined vision of this not very important process. And in doing so, they discovered some very important things. It turns out that corporate customers consider the account analysis process to be critical in their relationship with the bank. In fact, customers described the bank statement as a window into the back rooms of the bank (Figure 4-1). The errors and issues on their statements were, to the customer, merely artifacts and symptoms of the ills and failures of the bank's other internal functions and processes. During the CVM visioning, customers described a future

The *customer focus groups* revealed that the bank statement
serves as a *"window"* into the bank's operations and processes.

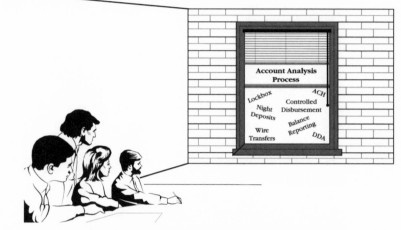

Customers' View Into the Back Rooms of the Bank

Figure 4-1 Selecting the right scope: Take the customers' viewpoint (© Copyright
IBM, 1999)

process that not only delivered value and differentiated the bank but
also maintained a bank image of having efficient and effective back
room processes. In other words, in the eyes of the customer, this
turned out to be one of the most critical bank processes.

Additionally, during the benchmarking portion of CVM, it was
learned that the bank's competitors felt this process could provide a
strategic advantage, and major banks in the market were investing
heavily to position themselves to be world class in this area.

Simply stated, this not very important process represented one of the
single most important areas for the bank to focus on to remain competitive. It became the ideal starting point and scope for developing a
customer-defined vision for business improvement and growth.

Developing the Right
Scope for a Customer
Vision

In Chapter 3, we discussed "whose view counts" as the first issue or
step in constructing the CVM vision pyramid. The next major step is

to identify and focus on the right scope of business activities and interactions with that customer segment. This includes identifying activities that directly touch and interact with the customer, which the customers feel are most important, and where value delivery could differentiate the company.

Focusing on a specific set of customer interactions for improvement and business investment is a critical scoping exercise. Effectively, this defines the field of play that the customer-defined vision will encompass. It can range from a focus on a small process of only a few steps (e.g., how a customer's account statement is created and delivered) to a broader focus across a business enterprise of several core processes (e.g., the full intracompany value chain from the order process through manufacturing, shipping and delivery, installation, and billing). The right scope for a customer vision in some cases may be to take an even broader view of a cross-enterprise value chain involving several companies. As an example, analyzing from the point where materials are acquired from suppliers, through how company processes manage individual orders, and on through distribution channels and third parties that manage outsourced activities, such as affinity programs.

Within that scope, the interactions between customers and the company's processes and services that create satisfaction or dissatisfaction are viewed as moments of truth (MOTs), which can be managed and leveraged to directly affect customer acquisition, retention, loyalty, and in turn, growth (Figure 4-2). In fact, CVM treats moments of truth as potential moments of value and strives to understand how value could be ideally delivered at each MOT.

Whatever field of play is defined, the focus will be on optimizing the value chain within that defined scope to deliver ideal, customer-envisioned value. A CVM analysis of a customer-defined scope of interactions will answer the question: How can we best leverage our position within this particular value chain to deliver benefits (value) to our targeted customer segments?

We will first discuss the three major fields of play (or scopes of vision) where CVM has been used to engineer ideal customer value delivery. Then within each of these scopes for business improvement, we will discuss the various MOT frameworks that need to be employed to craft a CVM customer-defined vision.

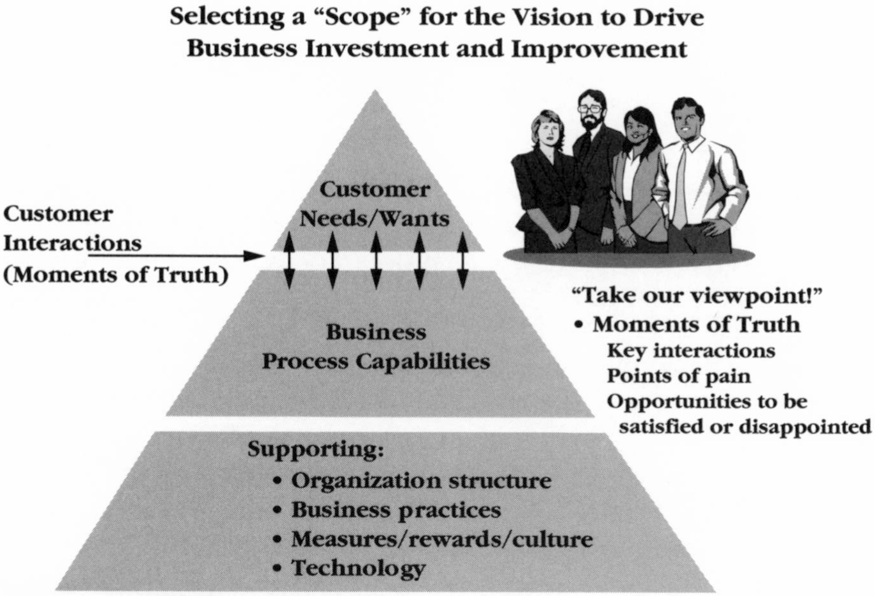

**Selecting a "Scope" for the Vision to Drive
Business Investment and Improvement**

Customer
Interactions
(Moments of Truth)

Customer
Needs/Wants

Business
Process Capabilities

Supporting:
• Organization structure
• Business practices
• Measures/rewards/culture
• Technology

"Take our viewpoint!"
• Moments of Truth
Key interactions
Points of pain
Opportunities to be
satisfied or disappointed

Figure 4-2 The next step in CVM: Selecting a focus area from the customer's perspective (© Copyright IBM, 1999)

Conducting Business on the Horizontal

Basically, there are three levels or scopes for horizontal business process analysis and business improvement:

- A single business process scope improving a process, such as billing.

- An enterprisewide scope improving a company across multiple processes, such as order process through manufacturing, delivery, billing, and postsales service.

- An extended-enterprise scope improving a multicompany value chain, such as the linkages from the company's external materials suppliers, through the company's internal order-through-invoice processes, and on through an external channel of distribution to the end consumer.

How wide a scope is needed for the vision? It depends on the problem being addressed.

Single Process Scope

A single process scope flows across numerous vertical functions within a company before producing an outcome that touches the customer (Figure 4-3). This single process focus may be appropriate:

- When customer dissatisfaction is localized to a particular process.

- When a company wishes to differentiate itself by providing high customer value with a specific customer-facing process.

- When a company is planning to spend money to improve a process for internal reasons (e.g., cost or defect reduction) and could also use that opportunity and investment to make the process more attractive to a targeted customer set.

- When a low-cost process or channel could dramatically reduce cost and increase profitability if only more customers could be attracted to use it (e.g., telephone banking or Internet-based e-business capabilities).

In these instances, the single process improvement scope and customer vision will include detailed microanalyses of customer interactions with a specific business process or service. (For example, how does a customer interact with a manufacturer's sales representative during the sales process?) The objective is to identify high-value customer needs, during those MOT interactions and then align the process capabilities with the customer needs that impact buying

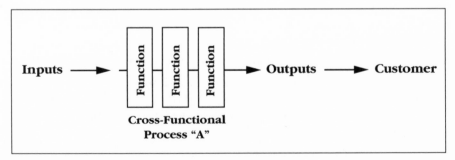

Figure 4-3 Process scope (single process)

behavior. The value chain being improved in this scenario is typically cross-functional and within the company. That is, several functions in the company may be involved in that process: administration, sales, pricing and contract management, manufacturing, and shipping, to name a few.

When an individual process is being improved, the MOT (value) analysis must be conducted at a very granular level. That's because customers will perceive a business process in terms of the many steps or activities required of them in association with this process. The company may perceive that there are only a few customer steps, activities, or MOTs, whereas the customer may perceive many. And by using CVM, each interaction with the process becomes an opportunity for satisfaction, value delivery, and delight rather than underperformance, disappointment, and dissatisfaction.

MasterCard: Developing a Single Process Vision. When MasterCard wanted to develop and implement a standard set of call center customer service standards, they utilized CVM and applied several of the concepts discussed in this book. To begin, they selected a single problematic (and high-opportunity) process: customer call center service. Second, they considered the segmentation of their marketplace and the several possible cardholder demographics (high-income, moderate, low-income; professional and nonprofessional; customers and noncustomers; East Coast, Midwest, South, West; etc.). Third, they considered both consumers and commercial customers. Fourth, they recognized that, beyond the cardholders, the member banks themselves were both channels and customers of MasterCard.

A basic CVM concept was then employed: To become an ideal provider to both their end user (the cardholder) and to their channel (the banks), MasterCard determined the consumers' needs and then enabled the banks to be the ideal channel to the consumer.

By identifying a customer-defined call center service vision (and the required process capabilities and infrastructure), MasterCard not only improved their own call center process but also shared this knowledge with the member banks, thereby enabling them to become ideal providers to their cardholder callers. In this manner, the integrity of the MasterCard brand and that of each banking channel member could be maintained. This was a classic win-win scenario.

In executing the project, MasterCard management initially hypoth-esized that there were four major MOTs for their call center cus-tomers:

- Calling for information (such as, what is your interest rate?).

- Calling for action (such as, change my address; raise my credit limit).

- Calling to order something (such as, send me a credit card appli-cation).

- Calling with problems and complaints (such as, I was billed incor-rectly!).

But when the CVM customer-visioning approach had the cus-tomers take an outside-in view, a more detailed picture quickly emerged. The customers perceived many more steps or MOT inter-actions. For example, suppose you are on vacation using a rental car and paying for it with your credit card. You understand that the card covers the collision liability on the rental car, but you want to know if it will also cover your college-age daughter if she is driving the car. A simple enough question, you think. Yet according to the cus-tomers, here are just some of the additional MOTs associated with that quest for information from a typical credit card service center. (Note: Their comments were generic for the industry and provided valuable insights into the marketplace view of "points of pain" with financial services and call centers.) A true, customer-centered com-pany welcomes this type of input, then acts on it:

- First, you have to go upstairs to get the telephone number.

- Then go downstairs and dial it.

- Then someone or something answers (e.g., automated voice response system).

- Then you are probably put on hold.

- Then you are asked for your customer number.

- So you hang up, go upstairs to the file, and get the customer num-ber.

- Then it's back downstairs to dial the number again.

- Then someone (or something) answers.

- Then you are placed on hold—again.
- Then you give them your customer number.
- Then they ask for some form of ID (e.g., Social Security number).
- Finally, they ask why you are calling.
- So now, at MOT number 13, you start to explain your inquiry.
- However, the answer requires specialized knowledge, so you are transferred to someone else for an answer.
- Then they ask what the problem is (at this point, your problem probably has little to do with your original inquiry).
- Nevertheless, you tell them that you are on vacation and rented a car with their credit card and understand that...

These steps were from real-life experiences recounted by cardholders (again, not attributed to any single credit card issuer). Clearly, the customers' view of the MOTs incurred during a call for information was significantly different than the initial internal view by company management, which was highly motivated and committed to competing on exceptional customer service. But as our other examples have cited, good management and good intentions are not enough. Customer value management arms those managers by providing them with an actionable customer view ("customer-defined points of pain" as MasterCard called them), which the company could then effectively eliminate by having the customers envision the ideal call center service provider.

In MasterCard's project, customers went on to develop their vision of the value they could receive at each moment of truth. In some cases, this involved eliminating certain moments entirely, such as having to repeat their issue or question after being transferred or after calling a second time. ("I should state my problem only once, and all future contacts should know and understand my issue!" was a typical piece of feedback from customers.)

Customers articulated the basic expectations that call centers must meet to retain their business. These became the basis for defining minimum call center service standards, which MasterCard could in turn provide to the banks as basic metrics. But for banks that wish to exceed basics or minimums and actually differentiate themselves and compete on service, the customers also defined an exceptional level that would delight them and attract their business. For example, customers stated a basic expectation that the first service person contacted should take ownership to get their question or issue resolved and that they should not have to restate their problem when talking to any subsequent service personnel. However, an exceptional level of service that would differentiate a call center was that the first point of contact would consistently have the capability to address customers' issues and questions during the initial contact. Once a full customer-defined vision of basic versus exceptional service was obtained, MasterCard then utilized CVM to develop an actionable vision of the specific call center process capabilities and infrastructure needed to deliver those service levels.

In summary, by making this single process analysis available to both MasterCard call centers and to bank call centers, both MasterCard and the channel were enabled to become ideal providers of benefits and value to consumers, driving growth for both organizations by leveraging a single high-impact business process.

Enterprisewide Scope

An enterprisewide scope covers a multitude of internal processes that make up the intracompany value chain and affect the products, services, or customer-facing processes that ultimately touch the customer (Figure 4-4). The enterprisewide scope may be appropriate under circumstances such as these:

- When a company wishes to compete on something other than product or price, it may do an enterprisewide analysis of its business processes to identify interactions (MOTs) with key processes that could be levered to create high customer value, differentiating itself on process or service value to customers. Companies may have the highest priced service or product, but thrive nonetheless because of the customer-perceived value of their collective processes and services.

- When a company is planning major infrastructure enhancements and expenditures, such as an I/T strategy or new salesforce automation, it could be done in a manner to make the company more attractive to customers. That is, while we have the engine compartment open for repairs and are investing in new parts for the business, why not assemble them in such a way that we also become more attractive to customers and grow market share?

- When a company is losing market share or has high customer attrition, it may need to do a cross-enterprise analysis to identify which business processes and services could be levered to remove inhibitors or customer dissatisfiers, thereby reducing attrition drivers. The same processes would also be analyzed to determine if competitors' offerings are providing high service value, thereby luring customers away from the company.

An enterprisewide visioning scope will include macroanalysis of customer interactions across the entire firm to identify the highest leverage processes for improvement and their related customer needs and wants during major MOT interactions. The performance capabilities of key processes (combinations of processes or a single identified highest leverage enterprise process) are then aligned to ideally deliver high-leverage customer needs or behavior drivers. The value chain being improved is typically cross-enterprise and multiprocess, that is, end to end from the order process through the delivery, installation, and billing processes.

For example, the credit card company could have elected to examine the entire set of customer interactions with their full set of enterprise business processes, including network operations, telephone service center processes, billing and collections processes, and outbound direct sales calls or cross-selling during inbound customer-initiated service calls. Each of these business processes can be charted or mapped out in MOT detail to determine where, from a customer viewpoint, value creation opportunities exist and which of the enterprise processes offer the greatest potential for reducing

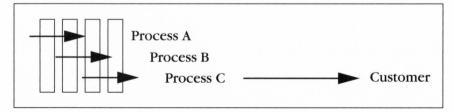

Figure 4-4 Enterprisewide scope (multiple processes)

customer dissatisfaction or increasing and driving customer loyalty and market share.

When enterprisewide customer-focused business improvement and growth are considered, the moments of truth (value) analysis is conducted at a higher level than with a single process. Customers perceive an enterprise in terms of major interactions that occur during the natural course of a relationship life cycle. From the company's viewpoint, these tend to group around the major customer-facing business processes, such as selling, installing, postsale service, billing, discontinuance, and so on. However, from the customers' perspective, these will be viewed in different terms:

- Company sell process interactions become buying or purchasing in the customer view.

- Company distribution process interactions become warehousing or receiving in customer terms.

- Company billing or invoicing process interactions become accounts payable.

This brings up two notable points of interest. First, as shown in Figure 4-5, when customer MOTs are analyzed at the enterprise level of analysis, they may be most easily understood and depicted as a life cycle for customer relationships. Classical Gas is a depiction of a gas company's customer life cycle, which begins with the customer's awareness of the company (possibly by interacting with the company's advertising, marketing and promotions, or sales processes) and then proceeds through several typical interactions with other company processes as the customer secures information and acquires products and services. Ultimately, after interfacing with other company processes such as service, billing, and so on, the customer either ends the relationship or continues (e.g., with repurchases) in an ongoing cycle of interactions.

The second notable point is that when the customers are commercial entities (other companies), the MOT analyses will reveal that the relationship between the two firms is actually a series of interactions between their respective business processes (Figure 4-6). Major opportunities are identified in Figure 4-6 to provide value to the customer. An important means to differentiate an enterprise and attract market share (growth) is depicted in this analysis to the extent

**Classical Gas Co. Customer's Life Cycle Was Used
to Identify the High-Level Major Moments of Truth**

Enterprisewide Scope:
Timeline of MOTs from
customer "awareness"
of company through
discontinuing customer
relationship

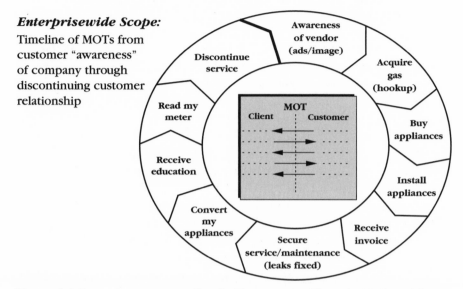

Figure 4-5 Enterprise moments of truth: The customer life cycle (© Copyright
IBM, 1999)

that the output of company processes can be designed to provide
ideal input to the customer's processes. By reducing the customer's
cost of doing business, for example, the company can differentiate
itself and enjoy preferred supplier status. In other words, the enterprise can be engineered to benefit its customer's ability to conduct

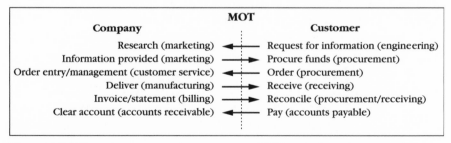

Figure 4-6 When the customer is a company: MOT analysis at the enterprise
level often depicts the customer processes that are interacting with company
processes

business. That is why applying CVM at the enterprise or extended-enterprise level is so powerful: There are so many opportunities to compete on service and service value delivery by improving the customer's processes.

Classical Gas: Looking Across the Enterprise for the Customer Satisfaction Levers. Classical Gas (not their real name) represents a textbook application of CVM. An old, established, single provider (read that, "monopoly") of gas to a major metropolitan area, Classical Gas was shaken by change: deregulation of the industry and the immediate entry of a formerly unknown entity—competitors. Classical had no idea how to respond. They were losing customers, yet they lacked basic customer acquisition and management capabilities. Their corporate lexicon did not even include the word *customer*. They spoke not of customers but of meters, as in, "How many meters do you have in your territory?"

So when competition arrived and their meters began to leave, Classical became concerned. "Where do we even begin?" asked a senior manager, looking at a wall chart depicting many lines of business, including acquisition and distribution of gas to residences and corporations, maintenance of a *distribution system* of underground gas lines, selling, installing, and servicing gas appliances. The geography was broad, the customer base huge and unsegmented beyond commercial and residential "meters," and the product line was virtually an undifferentiated commodity. The senior management team realized that reengineering of business capabilities and infrastructure was required to transform them into a customer-centered enterprise. They turned to CVM to formulate a customer-defined "to-be, end state vision." The scope of effort was determined to be enterprisewide, so the life cycle of a customer was used to define the MOTs. These moments were customer interactions with the key customer facing business processes at Classical.

The views of major customer segments were obtained regarding the relative business impact and importance of each interaction plus their perceived performance level. For the most important interactions (e.g., the repair of gas leaks in a timely and effective manner or the installation and maintenance of heating equipment), customer needs and wants were then identified (e.g., protect and ensure my safety, identify leaks and exposures and take preventive measures, or make repairs quickly, in one call, and restore my property to its original condition). (Note: How to secure such a customer vision and actionable needs and wants is covered in Chapter 5.)

Based on the customer-defined vision for the business at each major interaction point (sales process, installation process, postsale service process, emergency maintenance process, billing and invoicing process, etc.), the company was able to identify where the customers perceived the greatest performance gaps. These became opportunities for improvement, pinpointing specific processes for action, complete with the targeted markets' needs and wants as design points.

The end result was that Classical Gas was able to:

- Segment its marketplace based on customers with different needs.
- Design key business processes capabilities and infrastructure to deliver customer-defined value for the target customer segments.
- Remove inhibitors which had made its processes unacceptable and caused attrition.
- Add attractors which would differentiate its processes and generate growth.
- Reverse its customer dissatisfaction trend and position itself for the new era of unregulated competition in the utilities industry.

The company also discovered that it was missing a business process that would be critical to its viability and future success. An ongoing process for CVM would be required to monitor its customers' changing needs and wants continuously and to understand the implications on related company products, services, processes, and infrastructure.

Multicompany or Extended-Enterprise Scope

An extended-enterprise focus looks for opportunities to improve a multicompany value chain and can provide the greatest possible field of play to improve horizontal process efficiency, effectiveness, and value (Figure 4-7). An extended-enterprise, cross-company scope is appropriate when:

- A business wishes to team or form alliances, combining the core competencies or capabilities of multiple companies in order to collectively provide a product or service that cannot easily, or efficiently, be duplicated by the competition.

- A business wishes to reduce costs by rising above the many processes of its suppliers, itself, and its channels and by viewing their combined activities as a single value chain, which could have costs removed and efficiencies designed for all the parties if treated as a single entity.

- A business wishes to lever its channels, providing high-quality input to the channel, thereby making the channel ideal to the ultimate paying end user or consumer.

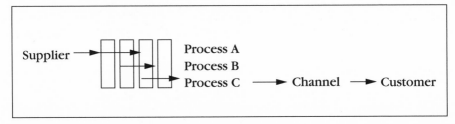

Figure 4-7 Extended-enterprise scope (full value chain)

A customer vision for an extended-enterprise scope can cover several companies. The value chain being improved is multienterprise and may be comprised of processes from within the company, its suppliers, alliances, channels, and (ideally) the end customer. The MOT (extended value chain interactions) analysis is conducted at a high level, similar to an enterprise-level study, as the interactions between companies in a customer value chain also tend to be between their major business processes. This offers an opportunity to redesign and improve the chain as a single entity focused on meeting the end consumers' requirements, while optimizing the piece-parts of individual companies and suppliers (Figure 4-8).

A CVM approach can be applied to improve any portion of the value chain or the full extended-enterprise chain. The correct customer view, or scope or breadth, will depend on the business issues that are being addressed. A cross-enterprise or extended-enterprise view covers a myriad of customer–supplier relationships (Figure 4-8):

Customer Value Management
Extended Enterprise — Full Value Chain Analysis

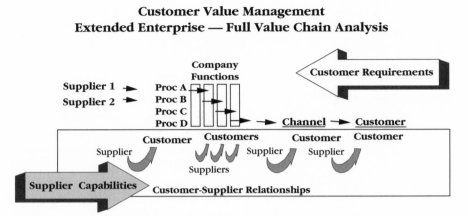

Figure 4-8 The ultimate CVM scope: Improving the full value chain, end to end (© Copyright IBM, 1999)

- Within a company process, the individual functions act in a horizontal customer–supplier capacity among themselves as work flows across functions to complete the process.

- Within an enterprise, the individual processes act in a customer–supplier mode as business activity flows cross-process.

- Within the complete value chain, one company serves as supplier to the next company (customer) in the chain until the final product or service is delivered to the end customer or consumer.

In the case of the credit card company, a different business issue or objective might have resulted in such a cross-enterprise, full value chain analysis. If the issue they were addressing had been customer satisfaction when actually using their credit card, for example, the study scope would have been extended to include the merchant's cash register point-of-sale procedures for securing card authorization and the approving member bank's role in that extended-enterprise, multicompany process. Taking such a view offers the most opportunity for improving end-to-end efficiency and overall customer satisfaction.

Typically, each individual firm in an extended value chain tends to view its role as a single localized process. Merchants might seek to improve their own point-of-sale credit approval procedures, for example, and the member banks might see their portion primarily as a risk management process to be optimized or as a simple internal financial ledger process. And without the CVM approach, a credit card company, as the network operator, might easily be focused on improving only its own portion as an electronic network operations process. From the customers' perspective, however, this is a single process: They're using their credit card. That's all! And if each player in that process took one minute to complete his or her subprocess, from the customer's viewpoint the total process might result in several minutes of standing, in embarrassment, while delaying the cash register line.

With CVM, virtually any player in a value chain who elects to conduct an extended-enterprise analysis has an opportunity to optimize their position in the chain by focusing on the end customer or consumer view. By taking the customers' point of view and determining the customers' desired ideal outcome, it may be possible to improve the overall value chain by treating it as a single multicompany process, improving customer satisfaction while potentially reducing costs for all participants.

L. L. Bean and Federal Express: Getting the Mittens to Granny.   An excellent example of applying this customer-centric CVM concept can be found in Freeport, ME. L. L. Bean defined its field of play or scope for business process management as extending from its suppliers, through its own processes and beyond, ending only at the ultimate consumer of L. L. Bean products. While many firms will closely manage customer orders from point of sale until the product leaves their shipping dock, L. L. Bean continues to manage the value chain until the product is actually received by a satisfied customer.

In other words, they have adopted the customer view and scoped their business vision and capabilities to align with the customer. From the customer perspective, the process is not the supplier manufacturing and shipment processes plus the Bean Company warehousing, inventory order management, customer service, picking, packing and shipping processes plus the trucking company pickup, central dispatching, distribution, and delivery processes (each of which, by the way, is typically viewed and managed individually by most industries today). From the customers' viewpoint, the process is the "get the mittens to granny by Christmas" process, and customer satisfaction and continued business success for everyone in the value chain hinge on that outcome!

As a result, L. L. Bean has partnered with Federal Express, and the FedEx processes have been integrated into the L. L. Bean processes. Due to this extended cross-enterprise process view, a call to L. L. Bean customer service inquiring about the status of the mitten order is responded to by telling the caller exactly where the package is in the delivery (subprocess) and when they might expect to receive it. L. L. Bean approaches the process as a single, integrated, multicompany process.

Wal-Mart and Pampers: Using an Extended-Enterprise View to Keep Diapers on the Shelves. Certainly, the most notable and notorious example of supply chain optimization from a cross-enterprise viewpoint was the integration of Wal-Mart's purchasing, warehousing, inventory management, and shelf-stocking/management processes with those of their supplier Procter & Gamble (P&G). A few years ago, Wal-Mart was experiencing difficulties keeping shelves stocked with Pampers, a popular disposable diaper. The result was costly in more ways than one: Customer satisfaction deteriorated, sales were lost, and there were numerous increased costs associated with inventory inefficiencies.

The solution was to rise above the current single Wal-Mart process of ordering more Pampers when supplies were low and then hoping P&G delivered them on time. Instead, Wal-Mart examined the entire value chain. By looking at the combined Wal-Mart and P&G processes as a single value chain, it became apparent that there was a better way. In the old setup, both Wal-Mart and P&G had their own inventory, ordering, shipping, receiving, and warehousing organizations. It wasn't unusual in this sea of redundancy that things fell through the cracks, such as orders to get Pampers to the stores quickly and efficiently.

Wal-Mart and P&G agreed that a better design was a single process that would reside in only one company. Wal-Mart would eliminate much of its own order, purchasing, receiving, warehousing, inventory, and shelf-management infrastructure, and P&G would redesign its own order fulfillment process to become responsible for shelf and inventory management for all Wal-Mart stores. In other words, it became the supplier's responsibility, not the customer's or channel's, to keep the right amount of inventory on the shelf, and costs were reduced for both parties. Essentially, Wal-Mart told P&G that they are the sole supplier for this particular product, and in being so, they had responsibility to design and implement the processes and systems that would keep the shelves stocked.

In the end, it was clearly a win-win solution for all, including consumers, who got what they wanted when they wanted it.

Financial Services Company: Extending the Enterprise and Opening a New Channel Without Alienating the Old One. Only a few years back, a major global financial services firm conducted a CVM analysis and developed business and technology strategies to position the company for the upcoming strategic period of the year 2000 and beyond. Their historic mission and vision were to provide superior financial services and support to a specific channel: independent financial advisers who, in turn, marketed investment opportunities to individual investors. Using a CVM approach, the company took an extended-enterprise view of its business and marketplace, exploring how it could be the ideal provider to the advisers who, in turn, wished to become the preferred provider of financial products, advice, and service to the marketplace.

By looking at the full value chain, it became apparent that the end customer investor must be the design point for a combined financial company and financial adviser delivery of value. To accomplish this, the needs and wants of high-value investor segments were determined and a customer vision was developed for these segments. Using the customer-defined vision of an ideal financial services provider, the company was able to identify the specific business processes and capabilities and infrastructure it must have to enable the advisers to be ideal to their investors. In this manner, they took an extended view of their business and invested to become ideal to their channel so that the channel, in turn, could delight the targeted end user or consumer.

In the course of the work, certain customer segments indicated a strong need for an alternative means of access to the company including, for some, direct access. These investors or prospective customers indicated that they did not need the advice, counsel, or services provided by the adviser channel. However, the customer vision developed by members of that segment indicated that they would value an ability to directly access and acquire certain financial products for themselves. As a result, the company vision and mission were expanded to include being ideal both to their channel (the financial advisers) and to their end customer (the investors). A new process for direct customer access was engineered and successfully implemented. This opened a new market for customers that the financial adviser channel simply could not reach because these customers preferred to deal directly with financial services companies. Since the appeal was to a customer set that the financial advisers weren't going to reach, the firm was able to expand its investment base without alienating their primary channel.

The CVM approach can help a company establish a strong channel relationship while also enabling direct customer access without damage to the channel. It provides a compelling analysis to assist channels with the segments that wish to deal via a channel by treating them in a manner that will boost those segments' satisfaction, retention, and loyalty. Additionally, they will have documented actionable needs and wants for other segments that prefer not to go through the channel and can reengineer their own company capabilities to provide direct access.

Whatever the Scope of the Vision, Optimize That (Value Chain) Scope by Designing to the Needs and Values of the End Customer

In each of these three alternative scopes (single process, cross-enterprise, multienterprise), the theme remains optimizing customer and supplier delivery of value by using the needs and wants of the customer to define and design the capabilities of the supplier. The application of this concept is probably most obvious in the single process example. The customer is most easily and visibly depicted at the end of the process as the recipient of specific process output (often expressed as services). In the simple single process example, however, the complexities discussed in Chapter 3 still exist regarding who is the customer and whose view, needs, and opinions are important to include in the vision.

On the other hand, the many customer–supplier relationships within an enterprise-level or an extended-enterprise-level business analysis can be less obvious and far more complex. Customer value management provides a crucial, systematic approach to unravel and harvest these relationships for high-leverage improvement opportunities. With rising customer expectations placing stress on all elements of the value chain, CVM has become a powerful approach to drive growth by using the customer view of value at either the process, enterprise, or cross-enterprise level.

After the Scoping: The Next Step

Once a customer segment has been targeted (Chapter 2), when whose view counts has been determined (Chapter 3), and once the appropriate scope and field of play for business analysis and improvement are defined (Chapter 4), the next step becomes the art and science of customer visioning. Reengineering your business capabilities to ideally align and link with customers' needs requires an actionable customer vision of an ideal you. How to secure such a view is covered in Chapter 5.

EXERCISE
Applying CVM to Your Business

Management Issues

What is your optimum scope of effort or focus for business improvement? What are the moments of truth (value) within that scope which are opportunities to create customer satisfaction or disappointment?

1. Process or enterprise improvement scope
   - What problematic customer-facing processes do you have? Which process receives the most negative customer satisfaction responses or complaints?
   - What are the moments of truth (microinteractions) within that process that are the customer-defined points of pain that could be improved?
   - Which processes could be leveraged to differentiate the firm with service value and attract market share?
   - What processes are targets for cost or defect improvement reengineering, which could be concurrently redesigned to be attractive to customers?
   - What major infrastructure improvements are planned (e.g., salesforce automation, call center equipment, etc.) that could also be designed to make the company more attractive to customers?
   - Which low-cost processes or channels do you wish to make more attractive to customers (or remove inhibitors) to increase usage?

2. Extended-enterprise or multicompany scope
   - What third-party channels could be leveraged by providing them with increased value from your processes or by enabling them to be ideal to their customers?
   - What supplier-through-channel multicompany processes could be leveraged by treating as a single process? How can your company benefit from its position in that integrated chain?

5

Value

Identifying Actionable
High-Leverage Customer Needs

They can have any color car that they want...
as long as it is black!

HENRY FORD

Recently, in a restaurant in Brussels, I was dining with friends and colleagues who were attending a seminar on CVM at our International Executive Education Center. The conversation was populated with picturesque stories that recounted how each dinner guest, as customers themselves, had personally experienced disappointing or bad service. It seemed that even in today's world, with all the emphasis on customers, businesses just do not appear to get it when it comes to providing good customer service. Everyone was having difficulty getting the kind of service they wanted.

The stories became more colorful as each person came up with an example that was even more outrageous than the last. Finally, one of the guests, who had been quietly listening, observed, "I don't know where you people do business, but I have to disagree. I have not had a really poor service experience in quite some time." The other members of our party quickly became agitated as each person strongly reiterated that they could not remember actually having a good service experience. The debate went back and forth for several minutes, and then I offered this hypothesis: Perhaps this person did not notice poor service because he had been conditioned to the point where he did not recognize it. "Maybe," I said, "not getting exactly what one wants is so common that it goes practically unnoticed!" The happy customer looked at me quizzically. I offered to demonstrate what I meant and stopped our waiter as he walked by. "My friends and I have theater tickets," I said, "and we need to leave immediately. We would like to pay you. We are in quite a hurry!" The words *immediately* and *hurry* were spoken with emphasis.

The waiter turned and rushed away.

"Now watch this," I said to my colleagues. "You are about to observe the first step in the end-of-the-meal process, and it is the same step no matter where you are in the world and no matter what you have just told the waiter regarding your urgency to leave the restaurant. The first step to settle your financials and secure your payment is always the same: He won't bring our bill; instead, he will clean the table!" Sure enough, the waiter returned in a few moments and began to remove the dishes and clean the breadcrumbs from the table.

"We really need to leave quickly," I reminded him. He nodded his understanding and then brusquely began to remove the cutlery from the table. He was in the end-of-the-meal process and was not going to deviate, no matter what I said to him. In fact, it became obvious that any further expression of my needs would be considered a distraction from his ability to do his job (which, ostensibly, was to serve me). This was an excellent restaurant and one that, no doubt, prided itself in providing superior service. However, service was defined in their own terms and had nothing to do with what the customer might value at any given moment. The level of service, as the restaurant defined it, was performed flawlessly, but the customer suffered. And I have seen this same scenario played out all over the world because I test it wherever I go.

Businesses in virtually all industries are repeating this vignette millions of times a day. They believe they know what is important, and they may in fact do those very things extremely well. However, while a supplier of electronics components may be congratulating itself for "efficiently cleaning breadcrumbs from the table," its most prized commercial customer may want something very different and may be looking for a supplier that will listen. In this case and in countless others, businesses are not hearing the voice of the customer.

Earlier in the book, I noted how customer expectations are set in ways companies cannot easily track. A hotel chain had its customers' expectations for service set higher because of superior service delivered by Hertz. As the hotel and Hertz example demonstrates, the desire to find a supplier that really listens to customers and never disappoints them is reinforced when customers deal with companies that do listen to them. And many of those companies are setting dramatically new performance expectations as they give their customers what they want, how they want it, when they want it! Because customers can get a specific appointment for at-home service on a Sears home appliance, they subsequently expect to get their automobile repaired at a specific time. After receiving a loaner Lexus while theirs is in the shop, they expect to receive a loaner computer while their laptop is being serviced. On automatically receiving their preferred newspaper at any Ritz Carlton they check into around the world, they expect their airline to remember their meal preferences. After having American Express customer service make an unsolicited offer tailored to a personal need, they expect all banks, insurance companies, and catalog retailers to demonstrate a similar knowledge of them in all subsequent contacts. After receiving expert advice rather than a sales pitch from a no-commission broker, they expect all retail salespeople to be trusted advisers rather than product pushers.

Similarly, commercial corporate customers are becoming conditioned to expect their vendors to understand how the business processes of the two companies interact and to take action to reduce not only the defects but also the cost and cycle time experienced by the customer–company processes. And in some cases, they expect the supplier to assume total responsibility for a multicompany extended process the way Wal-Mart assigns responsibility for maintaining its shelf inventory of disposable diapers to Procter & Gamble.

Obviously, the performance bar that a firm must be capable of jumping over to retain its customers is rising relentlessly. The challenge for business is to do two things:

- Understand what their customers value, especially as those values change constantly.
- Maintain an alignment between what customers' value and what the business is actually able to do.

Of course, this is not easy, because defining value depends on everyone's unique perceptions. Customer value management provides a way to understand customers' values and then leverage that knowledge to prevent customer dissatisfaction or to influence buyer behavior. In this chapter, we describe an approach to determine not only what a targeted customer set needs or wants but also what it values. Understanding customers' underlying values unlocks buyer behavior and opens the door to improved customer loyalty and market share.

A customer-defined vision can provide a company with a significant competitive advantage. Yet a common impediment to developing a customer-defined vision is the absence of a method to acquire actionable knowledge of rapidly changing customer needs. Companies continue to believe that they know their customers' needs based on past history, although customers' expectations are reset dynamically by daily interactions with other companies, often in completely different industries. This makes a strong case for developing some new ways to listen to customers and to use the voice of the customer to establish the design points for business processes.

Approaches to Listening

Businesses can have many different problems, goals, or objectives that drive their interest in developing a customer vision. That being the case, we will take two different approaches that, although not intended to be a "two-sizes-fit-all" framework, can cover most business issues. The first approach is to meet customer expectations, thereby reducing customer dissatisfaction and/or attrition. The second approach for customer visioning enables a company to exceed expectations, compete on ideal delivery of customer value, attract customers, and grow market share. One approach will effectively manage dissatisfaction by meeting expectations, whereas the other will go beyond that and manage loyalty and attract share by exceeding expectations to the point that a competitive advantage is created.

Let's begin with meeting expectations and managing dissatisfaction. Many companies do not wish to invest in infrastructure to perform beyond their customers' minimum acceptable expectations for services or for service value. These firms may have a strategy to be the low-cost provider, for example, and wish to compete solely on price as a commodity vendor. Other firms may want to focus on their customers' minimum acceptable level of service but for different reasons: They may have extremely poor customer satisfaction, hundreds of customer complaints, or excessive customer turnover and attrition. For the latter companies, quickly addressing customer-attrition issues may become a matter of survival. But for either of these, taking the time and expense to create a customer vision of ideal delivery of value would not be appropriate. What they need most is a simple framework to understand and manage the current delivery of their customers' minimum acceptable service standards.

Doctors Valarie Zeithaml, Leonard Berry, and A. Parasuraman developed a simple yet effective framework for customer satisfaction management. They conducted a multiyear study to determine the manageable elements that comprise how customers perceive service quality, which can help companies understand why they sometimes fail to deliver a satisfactory service level. This research and the associated findings are described in their book *Delivering Quality Service: Balancing Customer Perceptions and Expectations* (New York: Free Press, 1990).

Figure 5-1 depicts the alignment that must be present to manage or reduce customer dissatisfaction. A company's customer satisfaction surveys and internal performance standards, metrics, and measures of success must link to customer-defined needs and expectations. Once the company is correctly measuring the right things, by improving their performance on those items they can close the gap between what customers expect and what customers perceive they are receiving regarding those needs and expectations.

Simply stated, the framework explains the findings of the academic research:

- The gap between what customers expect and what they perceive has actually been delivered is measurable dissatisfaction (satisfaction equals expectation minus perceived performance).

- Further, they found that this satisfaction gap between expectations and performance, as perceived by a company's customers, could be explained by four parallel gaps occurring within the company:

  1. A gap between what customers expect and what the company thinks customers expect. For example, Zeithaml and associates

Managing to Expectations

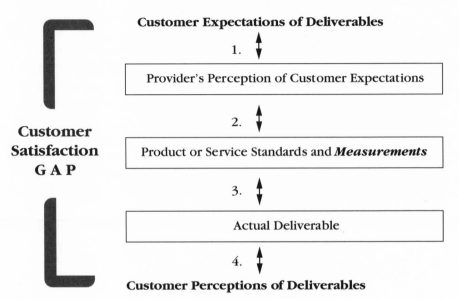

Figure 5-1 Meeting expectations: Customer dissatisfaction management (Adapted from Zeithaml/Berry/Parasuraman Framework)

cited focus group feedback where customers expressed concern that others could easily overhear their sensitive discussions with bank personnel or stockbrokers, whereas bank and securities brokerage executives were apparently oblivious to the importance attached by customers to transaction privacy. Many firms have internal perceptions of customer expectations that are simply off the mark.

2. A gap between what customers expect and the actual service standards and measurements that the company has established as internal metrics of success. Executives interviewed expressed frustration over an inability to translate their understanding of customers' expectations into service-quality specifications. Automobile service centers, for example, know that many customers would prefer to have work done on their cars while they wait. However, they may not be able to see how they can make that a measurable performance standard or design point for their business capabilities. Further, they do not incorporate

such customer-defined needs into their customer satisfaction surveys.

3. Gaps between the company's service standards and the actual performance delivered by the company, what Zeithaml and associates call *the service delivery gap*. The reasons for this may include the willingness, or lack thereof, of service personnel to perform to service standards, but most often it is because process capabilities or infrastructure do not enable attainment of the standards.

4. Finally, a gap between actual performance and what is communicated to the customer. Many companies perform to the levels expected by the customer or have improved performance but fail to communicate that to the customer, resulting in a customer perception of poor performance.

Additionally, if a company makes a promise for a specific level of service, especially if that promise is made in writing or via advertising, it had better keep that promise. The hotel chain I discussed in Chapter 2 promised a specific level of service (i.e., no surprises) but was unable to keep that promise. There was a huge gap between the customer's expectations as set by the hotel and what the hotel delivered.

These various gaps exemplify how business enterprises with the right intentions can fail when it comes to customer satisfaction. As stated earlier, good managers with good intentions sometimes aren't enough to remain competitive. You also need a systematic approach or framework for action.

The Zeithaml and associates framework for managing and minimizing customer dissatisfaction is eloquent in its simplicity. Using it to diagnose current high levels of customer dissatisfaction and to prescribe corrective action is relatively simple compared to developing and implementing a future vision to compete on ideal delivery of exceptional service value.

The company must first identify the customers or customer segments it wishes to focus on to minimize dissatisfaction or reduce attrition. Then the firm must make an overt decision to compete for this segment based on meeting must-have expectations versus differentiating exceptional service delivery or value. This may be due to an overall low-cost-provider company strategy, or it may be because the particular customer set is of relatively low value to the company and does not warrant either an investment in overperformance to retain them or a high-cost service infrastructure. The intent, under these circumstances, is to understand and meet only minimum expectations.

Next, the moments of truth interactions with this customer set must be examined and scoped. Is the concern focused at an enterprisewide level, with all the interactions between the company's customer-facing processes (sales, order, distribution and delivery, billing, accounts receivable, and postsales service)? Or is the concern a particular problematic process (customer service)? The field of play must be defined from the customers' viewpoint. Often, internal sources may be used to make this determination, such as customer complaint logs, customer opinion surveys, and front-line employees who can serve as customer advocates identifying the hot spots. These internal sources are useful in that they have firsthand knowledge of many of the customers' current issues. (Internal employees are also an excellent starting point for zeroing in on high-leverage issues and dissatisfiers to start an expectations-based dissatisfaction management framework. However, it would be inadvisable to use internal employees in our later examples of developing ideal customer-defined strategic visions.)

The moments of truth interactions from the customers' perspective are often the points in time they view as points of pain. For that reason, the company employees' input should be treated merely as hypotheses to be validated by the external customers. It is the customers themselves who must say at what level of detail (enterprisewide; single process; individual process interaction, activity, step) a company must set its sights in order to address perceived points of pain.

Some techniques to define these points specifically and to obtain the customer view (expectations regarding product or service process delivery) include:

- Customer complaint vehicles, such as 1-800 hot lines, customer reply cards, or Internet-based feedback systems.

- Interviews with front-line, customer-facing personnel (although these will reveal only things the customers are complaining about not receiving; they will not provide a full listing of all the customer expectations, many of which a company may be performing well).

- Interviews with customers who have recently defected.

- Interviews with recent lost bids (prospects who selected a competitive vendor).

- Focus groups with segments of customers who appear to have similar needs. (Although focus groups are used in later examples of future ideal value visioning, they may also be used to understand current dissatisfaction.)

- Customer satisfaction surveys, particularly if there are blank spaces on the survey for write-in comments to identify issues or unmet expectations. Note: An effective customer survey will normally require that many of the foregoing steps have already been completed. Otherwise, the survey may not be asking the right questions regarding things that customers have defined as being important or expected.

These steps will provide customer input that addresses the first gap in the Zeithaml and associates framework: alignment between what customers expect and the company's understanding of what customers expect. That, in turn, enables the company to address the second gap in the framework: alignment between what customers expect and the related product and service standards that the company has established as internal metrics of success.

A process to continuously compare customer-defined service standards versus company performance levels, plus management disciplines to identify and remove root causes of underperformance, will address the third potential gap in the framework: alignment between customer-defined service standards and the performance and delivery of services. For example, a company must continuously monitor its promises of service versus its ability to deliver. In the case of the hotel chain's promise to deliver against a zero defects standard, a process is required whereby each room in the hotel is regularly checked to ensure that the lights, television, and other systems work. Additionally, an infrastructure is required to address potential gaps in service quickly (e.g., fix a broken television or thermostat in a hotel room before a guest finds it).

A communications process or formal procedure to keep the customers informed of service delivery will address the fourth gap in the framework: alignment between company performance and the customers' perception of what is being delivered. Some automotive dealers and repair services, for example, routinely send postservice follow-ups to remind customers of the service received, while also asking if the work was performed to their satisfaction. Equally important, these businesses are committed to addressing any short-falls the customers identify.

Cumulatively, by managing these four company gaps, the fifth critical gap is effectively managed on the customer side of the equa-tion: customer satisfaction (the difference between what customers expect and what they perceive was delivered). In so doing, the issues of customer dissatisfaction and attrition may be managed and reduced.

The corrective actions that management may need to take to resolve the measurable customer dissatisfaction will normally revolve around adjustments to the company capabilities and infra-structure. These same approaches for business capabilities engi-neering will also be used to implement improvements indicated by our next framework for discussion: techniques to develop an ideal customer-defined vision. In the case of the Zeithaml and associates framework, however, any subsequent business engineering changes will be primarily focused on an objective of (and costs associated with) efficiently meeting, rather than dramatically exceeding, cus-tomers' expectations.

Plastics Company: Meeting Minimum Customer Expectations for a Commodity. A major plastics company was developing an informa-tion technology (I/T) strategy to position itself for the upcoming five-year period. The firm was concerned with the rising level of negative feedback and complaints on its customer satisfaction sur-veys; one element of the strategy was that the company's I/T should facilitate increased customer communications and, ideally, increased customer satisfaction.

Plastics are typically viewed as a commodity. The industry is seen as a price-based competitive environment, and this company had very competitive prices. Nevertheless, the company was still con-cerned with the possibility of losing customers due to factors other than price (e.g., ease of doing business, knowledge of the salesforce, etc.). The company knew that positive benefits from processes and services can provide high value, differentiate a company, and attract customers. At the same time, poor processes and the related performance will almost always drive customers away, especially in a commodity environment where prices are relatively equal. The plastics firm was content to offer product and price as their value proposition; however, they were not content to allow a negative value proposition from a process or service, such as unreturned phone calls or unknowledgeable sales representatives, threaten their customer base.

For this company, the customer segments were clearly known and understood; they had extensive knowledge of what their segments were and whose view counts. What they did not have was a clear customer view from those parties of their minimum expectations (i.e., gap 1 in the Zeithaml and associates framework for managing to expectations), which could be used to align their process and service capabilities, infrastructure, and metrics of success.

The new I/T strategy would need that critical input if it were to enable an improved customer focus. Rather than pursue a customer-defined vision of the ideal future plastics supplier processes, since they were not going to compete on process value, the firm elected to use the CVM approaches that are more geared to understanding their customers' must-have needs.

To secure the relevant customer view for this company, the CVM experts utilized several sources of information, such as company complaint vehicles to identify clusters of common issues and trend lines of occurrences. Specifically, they looked at:

- Customer surveys, including write-in comments that were extracted and clustered into groupings of common problems.
- Front-line employees, who were facilitated in workshops as customer advocates regarding apparent customer points of pain.
- Recent customer defectors, along with customers who did not award bids to the company.

Finally, hypotheses were developed of what the most important must-have needs were, including which needs were most often not met or in need of improvement. These were validated in interviews with key customers. In a matter of only a few weeks, the company had a focused customer vision of the expectations that it must meet to remain a viable supplier. This became the basis for subsequent I/T strategy and business process improvement to ensure they met the expectations of their target market. For this scenario, the Zeithaml and associates framework provided a simple and eloquent approach.

Exceeding Customers' Expectations (Competing on Process and Service Value to Attract Share and Grow)

Unlike the plastics company, most firms cannot stop at meeting expectations to manage customer dissatisfaction. In today's competitive environment, firms must look for new ways to differentiate themselves, attract share, and grow. Often, this differentiation comes in the form of understanding and delivering high customer benefit or value during process and service interactions (e.g., car rental companies eliminating waiting lines or airlines using ticket-free boarding systems).

Even firms with strong product and price value propositions can strengthen their position and become harder to copy by adding process and service benefits to their customer value portfolio. This is especially true for firms where product and price are close to that of the competition. To be a player (combatant) in this arena requires new management skills, tools, and techniques. It requires new ways to develop a customer view of exceptional value delivery and, more important, to understand which values actually drive customer buying behavior.

Such a framework to understand the behavioral impacts of different articulated needs was developed by Dr. Noriaki Kano from the Science University of Tokyo. Dr. Kano conducted research to understand how 50 companies could influence and manage customer satisfaction, not simply measure it. His resulting framework demonstrates a phenomenon observed during this study:

- The companies were able to identify many customer needs.
- All the customer needs were not of equal importance, nor do all have an equal impact on the business.

- Customer needs could be placed into a hierarchy of three tiers (Figure 5-2).

- The bottom tier was basic needs or expectations, which if not received, resulted in dissatisfaction. Kano referred to these as having only a one-way effect on customer satisfaction; that is, if they are not provided, it results in dissatisfaction. However, since they are "expected," providing them does not also drive increasingly higher levels of satisfaction. They have only one impact on satisfaction: If not provided, satisfaction declines. They become dissatisfiers.

- The next tier Dr. Kano observed was more directly linked to increased satisfaction in that it exceeded expectations. He observed a linear relationship between the performance of these items and satisfaction. They have a two-way impact on satisfaction: The more they are performed or provided, the proportionally greater is customer satisfaction, and vice versa.

- The third, or top, tier in the Kano framework is referred to as "exciters/delighters." As with the basic expectations, these have only a one-way impact on satisfaction. However, whereas basic needs only drive dissatisfaction if not provided, the exciter/delighter category only drives satisfaction if performed or provided. These are unexpected; therefore, if not provided, they do not result in dissatisfaction. Further, unlike satisfiers, they are nonlinear. That is, the value provided is so great that performance improvement results in greater than proportional satisfaction improvement. These are true satisfaction levers.

Dr. Kano's observations regarding the properties of this three-tier customer needs hierarchy were eye-opening. All customer needs are not equal. Beyond simply having the customers rank and prioritize their needs, we reasoned, another business metric was possible: categorizing needs and wants based on the actual impact they can have on buyer behavior. This could result in customer-defined investments to fulfill a business strategy via CVM:

- A business strategy to differentiate and compete on either low cost or on high customer value can be implemented by understanding a hierarchy of customer values and needs that drive their buying behavior.

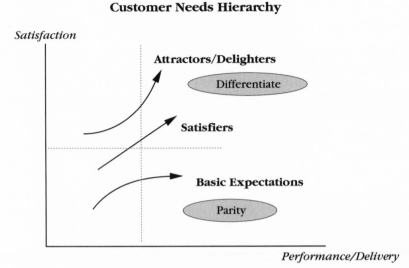

Figure 5-2 Exceeding expectations: Customer buying-behavior management
(Adapted from work by Dr. N. Kano, Science University of Tokyo)

- Customer behavior-driver needs (the value proposition) can be determined for each targeted market segment or for targeted segments of one.

- The needs and values can be prioritized based on the company's competitive strategy and the buyer values and behavior they wish to lever. If competing on low cost, the company would want to understand the basic must-have needs that the low-cost products, services, and processes must satisfy. But if competing on value provided by products, processes, and services, then exciter/delighter needs must also be understood to differentiate the company by providing high-leverage, behavior-driving quality or value.

- Additionally, customer-articulated needs which do not drive their actual behavior (do not cause customers to leave nor attract their business) can be identified and eliminated from the business design to reduce cost without impact on business volume.

To operationalize this powerful concept, CVM has modified and adapted Dr. Kano's hierarchy (Figure 5-2). The primary distinction is CVM's focus on understanding and managing the customers' buying behavior rather than their generic satisfaction. Customer value management concepts for securing a customer-defined view to do this are:

- Basic needs are bottom-tier customer requirements, which, if not met, result in catastrophic dissatisfaction and customer defections. Failure to provide these will cause the customer to leave, driving attrition and loss of market share. These are must-haves that define the minimum level of performance that a company must meet to be a qualified vendor. They are a company's ticket to play and define the entry-level business capabilities required to be a player in that industry, such as accurate bank statements or being reachable by telephone during standard hours.

- The next tier of needs is satisfiers, which, if met, exceed basic expectations but do not individually impact buyer behavior. These, in effect, put smiles on customers' faces, such as someone at the bank knowing the customer's name. They influence how the customer feels about the firm. But if not provided, the absence of these would not cause customers to leave, and if provided, they would also not individually attract a competitor's customer to change vendors. They may drive satisfaction, but not behavior.

- The top tier, exciters/delighters, provides such high or unexpected value that it would affect buying behavior and motivate a customer to change vendors to acquire it, although basic needs were already satisfactorily met. These are attractors or differentiators, in CVM terminology, because they can differentiate a company and attract and grow market share based on the value provided, such as having business processes that reduce the customers' cost of doing business.

The expectation-driven framework provided by Zeithaml and associates to manage and prevent dissatisfaction and the adaptation of Dr. Kano's framework to understand buyer behavior drivers provided CVM practitioners with two distinctive ways to view customer needs and to use this knowledge for business improvement. However, we still felt limited and constrained by what the customers were specifically able to tell us. And the Kano observations, while compelling, failed to show how to put the model into real-world application. He confirmed that the phenomenon of tiered customer needs existed, but not how to operationalize them or how to envision new ones that did not currently exist.

Ideal Value Delivery: Developing a Vision of What Does Not Exist

Many users of market research complain of an inability to get beyond what currently exists and develop customer requirements for things the customers themselves may not be aware of. A commonly cited example is the Sony Walkman. If Sony had relied solely on focus groups to envision their new products, skeptics say that the customers would never have come up with a requirement for a nonexistent audio/video product that can be clipped to their belt or worn on their head. The primary criticism is that the traditional focus group cannot look forward and envision that which does not currently exist. ("They tell us what's right or what's wrong, but say nothing of what can be.")

We needed a more robust method of gathering customer needs that provided a more actionable forward-looking view than normal focus group research. I once read that the *underlying value* provided by products and services is what creates the demand—and therefore the market—for them. It seemed to us that understanding the Kano categories (modified to reflect buyer-behavior impacts) and the underlying value or benefit of the customers' needs (which creates demand and a market) were the keys to market success.

Our breakthrough in using the voice of the customer to drive business process improvement had to do with moving from merely securing customer-articulated needs to understanding and leveraging the underlying value that customers receive from those needs. We reasoned that if our customer research could get beyond what customers say they want and begin to focus more on why they want it (the benefits or value of receiving it), it might be possible to operationalize the Kano framework. By having targeted customers develop a vision of ideal delivery of value, which would attract them to a company or service, we could differentiate the company and attract market share. We moved from focusing on what they want to why (i.e., the underlying value). It then became possible to work with customers to develop a customer-defined vision of what it would take to provide ideal delivery of value that may not exist today, attract share, and grow.

What we needed was a methodical approach to get to the underlying value proposition that was possible for each customer interaction.

Hitting Paydirt: Finally Hearing the Voice of the Customer

The breakthrough occurred at an unexpected moment during a focus group. A segment of business travelers was being facilitated regarding picking up a rental car. The facilitator was focusing on one moment of truth, specifically the point in time when the rental car courtesy bus drops the customer off at the rental car.

The facilitator asked, "What do you expect at this moment? What do you need? What do you want?" The customers shifted in their seats and no one answered this seemingly pointless question, but the facilitator persisted, "Work with me on this. We want to make each of these interactions between you and the rental car firm as optimum for you as possible. What would it take at that moment to be ideal?"

Finally, one customer replied, "I'd like a light on the side of the bus."

The facilitator said, "Fine, a light on the side of the bus," and wrote that phrase on a flip chart. But instead of proceeding to generate as many similar brainstorming ideas as possible, she asked, "Why?"

The customers looked at her. No one spoke.

"Why?" she repeated. "Why is this important to you at that particular moment?"

"Because," someone answered, "it's dark out there." Everyone laughed.

"Why is that important to you?" she asked again.

"Because," another person answered, "we are often at major airports."

"In major cities," said someone else.

"At remote rental car parking locations," said another.

"In high crime areas!" said a final voice, completing the thought.

"So what is the value of a light on the side of the bus? What is the benefit of it to you?" she asked.

"Personal security," said one customer.

"A sense of safety and relief from anxiety," answered another.

"Then forget the light," stated the facilitator. "Tell me what would be the ideal possible delivery of safety, security, and relief from anxiety that you could experience at that moment!" She was no longer focusing on what they wanted (the light) but instead focusing on why and the value they could potentially receive (safety, security, freedom from anxiety).

After a pause, one fellow replied, "Valet rental car...bring the car to me...I will stand where it is light and actually be safer, more secure, and freer from anxiety than if I were on a bus with a light on its side." Other customers quickly joined in and began to envision many different ways their common values could be provided other than by the light. "I'll go directly from the plane to the terminal exit, and the car will be there curbside," said one customer. "With my luggage in it!" another exclaimed.

And in that moment, customer visioning of ideal value delivery was born and integrated into our business process reengineering methods and customer value management.

By combining several such approaches (Zeithaml and associates, Kano, value visioning, etc.), powerful new techniques became possible to populate the top of the CVM pyramid with a customer-defined view or vision to assess and engineer business capabilities and infrastructure. The approach that is actually used should depend on the business issues, goals, and objectives, that is, to reduce customer dissatisfaction and attrition or to differentiate, attract new customers, and grow (Figures 5-3 and 5-4).

For example, when the company is attempting to reduce costs without losing customers, the approach in Figure 5.3 would be appropriate to identify and implement a business design intended to minimize defections. And of course, when a firm is losing customers at a high rate, these methods will isolate the issues. Managing and preventing customer dissatisfaction or attrition require understanding customers' basic needs at each major interaction. This approach may also be used when a company wishes to provide minimum services to identified low-value customer segments. Other situations might include looking for quick hitters to remove inhibitors that are preventing consumers from using a low-cost process; by addressing these barriers or inhibitors, the firm might increase the use of their least cost process, service, or channel.

CVM — Using Zeithaml et al. Framework

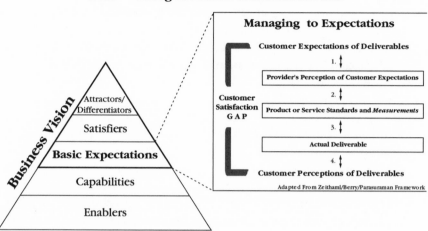

Figure 5-3 The CVM pyramid: Using a customer view to manage dissatisfaction and attrition (© Copyright IBM, 1999)

CVM — Using Kano Framework

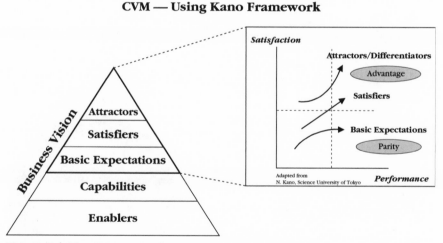

Figure 5-4 The CVM pyramid: Using a customer view to manage buyer behavior, attract market share, and grow (© Copyright IBM, 1999)

A compelling use of CVM is to go beyond understanding and removing mere inhibitors and dissatisfiers. Managing customer loyalty and growing market share are possible by identifying the customer value proposition and behavior drivers that differentiate you and actually attract customers. By combining a Kano-like behavior analysis and the CVM approaches to develop a customer-defined vision of ideal value delivery, high-leverage value propositions can be placed at the top of the value management pyramid (Figure 5-4). Subsequent infrastructure investments can be prioritized based on their anticipated buyer reaction and bottom-line results, as discussed in Chapter 6. This might be used where the company wishes to become more attractive to targeted high-value customer segments (by identifying their top-tier needs), while minimizing investments in low-value customer segments (by identifying and providing only their bottom-tier needs).

Whichever framework is utilized, however, the customer vision should target and define a desired future state that will fulfill the business strategy and provide a competitive advantage (Figure 5-5). The customer needs must be identified at an actionable level that will allow them to become design points for business engineering. For example, it is not actionable for a customer satisfaction survey to say that customers are unhappy with invoice accuracy. What are the customer-defined attributes and specific design points expected of an accurate invoice? Without these, no meaningful process improvement actions are possible.

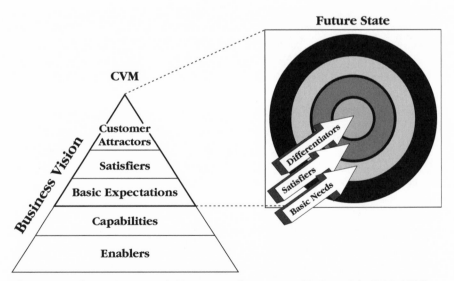

Figure 5-5 The CVM pyramid: Targeting a future state (© Copyright IBM, 1999)

IBM and a Large Commercial Bank: Getting the Customer to Define Accurate. One of the hardest things to secure is an actionable customer vision, and the reason is that (as with our prior examples) companies continue to believe they know what customers want or what customers mean. This is an almost universal truth. And given the rate of change in today's marketplace, companies are very often wrong.

Consider the complex relationships and myriad interactions between a major corporation (say, an IBM or a large commercial bank) and its commercial customers (selling and buying, shipping and receiving, servicing and being serviced, invoicing and paying, to name a few.) During the many micromoments of truth for each of those macroprocess-level interactions, the commercial customers have many different needs, wants, and expectations. And all of these require intimate knowledge of who, what, when, where, and how customers want things. And each of these will have to satisfy each individual customer's personal preferences and underlying needs. All in all, this offers many opportunities for misunderstanding, misalignment of business capabilities and measurements, and customer dissatisfaction.

But how common are these misunderstandings or misalignments? Many of the corporate executives I meet express a staunch belief that, having been in the business for 20 years, they know what their customers want. For example, when they look at a customer satisfaction survey and see a nonspecific factoid such as 34 percent were moderately satisfied, 27 percent extremely satisfied, and 39 percent were dissatisfied with invoice accuracy, they believe they know just what that means. But do they? Remember all the complexities of the hundreds of moments of truth and the potential for many different needs at each of those moments? Let's just look at one moment and one simple customer need. The moment is receipt of an invoice. The need is for invoice accuracy. What does that mean? This one example eloquently reveals the challenge and difficulty in developing an actionable customer vision.

Both IBM and a large commercial bank each wanted to understand and ensure customer satisfaction regarding the accuracy of their financial statements or invoices. Both corporations, being customer focused, utilized regular customer satisfaction surveys. However, both initially lacked sufficient customer input to make their satisfaction survey feedback actionable. An immediate conclusion drawn by both companies from negative surveys was that the prices on the statements or invoices must be incorrect. This generated an immediate focus on their billing systems and data to ensure the files reflected current and correct prices. In fact, both institutions felt they had an intuitive understanding of this customer issue.

Fortunately, IBM and the bank each commissioned a customer-defined vision of the ideal invoice or statement, and once again, the results were eye-opening. The bank's customers envisioned a lengthy list of attributes of the ideal bank statement, which of course included correct charges. However, there were many additional attributes of accuracy that the customers must experience in order to satisfy their minimum requirements, much less meet their vision of ideal. Two customer-defined billing statement requirements will suffice to make the point:

- An accurate statement must reflect the customer's full relationship. Therefore, if multiple statements are received, although the charges on them may be technically correct (priced right), each statement is considered inaccurate because it does not reflect all transactions with the bank.

- An accurate statement must have the same "as of" or cutoff date for all the types of charges appearing on it so that the customers can determine their complete financial status as of a single day. Therefore, if a bank practices batch processing at month's end, does checking account balances on Friday night, and other accounts or charges (lock boxes, international wire transfers, etc.) on Saturday, then in the eyes of the customer the statement is inaccurate.

The IBM customers' vision of an ideal accurate invoice also had many attributes of accuracy, including current and correct prices. However, many additional requirements were identified that had little to do with their billing process price file. Again, two will suffice:

- An accurate invoice also must facilitate ease of reconciliation by the customer. For example, customers cited how American Express attaches the original authorization (a copy of the charge slip signed at a restaurant) which easily validates the accuracy of the statement (self-validating accuracy). Therefore, if a technology firm has global sources for complex products, with varying lead times for different components, and customers have difficulty matching the multiple staggered invoicing to a single purchase order, they will perceive the invoices (although technically priced correctly) as inaccurate.

- An accurate invoice must match the original deal. In the mind of the customer, the fact that an invoice correctly reflects the current price is irrelevant. It should instead reflect the price that was quoted originally. Therefore, if a firm has a complex product line, contracts, and pricing, the proposal process becomes a critical part of the invoicing value chain, and merely reengineering the billing process will not ensure customer-perceived invoice accuracy.

The bottom line: Neither the bank nor IBM could have taken action to ensure high customer satisfaction with invoice accuracy had they not conducted the CVM work to get a clear, actionable customer-defined vision of what constitutes an ideally accurate invoice. And invoice accuracy is likely to be as simple (or intuitively understood) a customer need as you will experience.

There is no substitute for the voice of the customer. The small relative expense required to secure an actionable customer view, especially if it includes a future view of ideal delivery of value and buyer behavior drivers, pales in comparison with the expenditures that you will be making in business improvement and infrastructure. If you are going to make financial outlays to improve your infrastructure, processes, and services, why not do it the right way and make them attractive to customers?

Properly executed, the CVM approaches covered in this chapter provide the ideal input for the next step, prioritizing and targeting specific customer needs and values for business improvement and investment. In Chapter 6, we discuss how to take a customer-defined vision and move it from an undisciplined wish list to a rational set of business improvement priorities.

EXERCISE
Applying CVM to Your Business

Management Issues

How do your mission, vision, strategy, goals, and objectives align with the needs and behavior drivers of your target customers? How could an actionable customer vision be used to improve business performance?

1. Managing customer dissatisfaction or attrition
   - Do you compete on product or price and wish to provide only minimum required services? What are they? What do customers expect at each MOT?
   - Are your measurements and standards aligned with customer expectations?
   - Are your actual performance and deliverables meeting those standards?
   - Are you communicating positive performance attainment to the customer?
   - Are advertisements and other communications setting realistic customer expectations (is there alignment between your promises and capabilities)?
   - Do your surveys ask satisfaction on things that are important to the customer?
   - Which customer needs are the critical few that must be met?
   - What three to five things would most impact total satisfaction?

2. Managing buyer behavior and loyalty
   - Are your products and price relatively similar to those of the competition?
   - Do you wish to differentiate and compete on processes and services value?
   - What are your targeted customers' basic must-have needs?
   - What are your targeted customers' attractor differentiating needs?

- What underlying value could you exploit or deliver at each MOT interaction that your customers can ideally envision?
- What would make low-cost channels more attractive to your customers?
- How can you enable your customer to provide ideal value to their customer?
- What process differentiators would attract high-value customers?
- How can you retain low-value customers, but provide only low-cost basics?

6

Prioritization

Making Investment Decisions
Based on Buying Behavior

World-class at everything? Not in my company!
I only want to be the best at the critical few things
that will have a direct effect on my bottom line!
FINANCIAL SERVICES CEO

Once I was meeting with the CEO of a major financial services company who wanted his firm to become the preferred provider of such services to his customers. That's not a bad vision; however, he did not know what his customers valued most from financial services or what changes might be required. I explained that CVM was designed to accomplish such an objective and told him how it was possible to obtain the customers' vision of his company as an ideal vendor and then make that the design point for business investments and improvements. He nodded his approval, so I continued that we could also do a best practices study to identify examples of the business capabilities and infrastructure that enable world-class firms to excel at meeting those needs.

The CEO literally came out of his chair, pointed his finger at me, and said, "Be very careful using that phrase [world-class] around here. I do not want our employees thinking they must be world-class at everything. I only want to be the best at the critical few things that will have a direct effect on my bottom line!"

He was absolutely correct. You do not want to invest or strive to be world-class at fulfilling every customer need. A return on investment to meet many of those needs in a best-of-breed or world-class manner is not practical. Answering the telephone is a perfect example.

Answering the telephone is a very elementary customer requirement for your business. If you do not answer the telephone when customers call, they will not be your customers for very long. However, if you invest several million dollars to answer the telephone faster than any company in the world—say, in one ring—would that cause the customers of your competitors to abandon their former vendors and rush to do business with you? Probably not. Basic expectations, such as answering your phone in a reasonable number of rings, are simply expected to be provided. If those expectations are met, your company is then considered a qualified vendor. If they are not met, then you are considered unqualified. If you exceed such expectations in a world-class manner, that is irrelevant because overperformance of this type of need provides neither significant incremental customer value nor competitive advantage.

On the other hand, reducing the cost of doing business with your company and providing access to critical information are examples of things that, if performed exceptionally well, could provide significant incremental value to your customers. Rather than how quickly you answer the phone, the value proposition during a telephone contact may reside more in your customers' ability to receive actionable information or to reach a knowledgeable person the first time they call. Whatever the specific incremental value, the greater the level of your performance for this type of need, the greater its value to customers. The greater the value it delivers to customers, the greater its power to differentiate you and induce the customers of competitors to move their business to you.

Customer value management prioritization criteria rely heavily on such Kano-like concepts and consider both the customer's viewpoint (the customer-defined importance and performance levels of each need) and also the company's point of view (the potential impact on buying behavior and the relative performance gaps with competition):

- How important is a need to a customer?
- How important is that same need to the company?
- How well does the company perform versus the competition?

- Which need, if performance delivery improved, would most impact the bottom line?

Companies today are concerned with how to take a rapidly growing set of customer needs or expectations and develop a rational set of business improvement priorities that will have a direct effect on the bottom line. Just as the CEO forcefully told me, the issue is to avoid indiscriminate spraying of scarce resources and world-class services across all customers and to meet all customers' needs. No one can afford to be world-class at everything.

Of course, the question is: Which customer needs have the most impact on your business? This is especially difficult to answer in an environment where:

- Competitive offerings seem to change daily, and there is growing customer unrest or dissatisfaction with current products and features.

- Customer service centers increasingly are asked for more tailored, personalized service delivery.

- Trade journals regularly identify new combatants poised to enter the marketplace, as traditional industry borders dissolve and begin to merge (e.g., banking, insurance, and financial services mergers), which create new possibilities for product and service delivery.

- Broadcast and print media alike bombard the marketplace with predictions that the Internet will provide business with unprecedented customer-access flexibility (both access to customers and access by customers).

This translates to a buyers' market. Each company must visibly contend with, and meet or exceed, their competitors' capabilities to provide customers with increased benefits at a very personalized level. Such outstanding service or value delivery by one supplier or industry will breed new, higher customer expectations as they subsequently deal with all industries. (Remember, the faster you pick up your rental car from Hertz, the shorter you expect the check-in line to be at the hotel registration desk.) Bottom line to all this: Customer expectations will continue to rise. And fast.

From a management point of view, the marketplace appears to be a cacophony of upward-spiraling customer needs, wants, desires, complaints, requirements, predictions, and forecasts. The challenge is to take this undisciplined customer wish list and convert it into a more rational set of business investment priorities.

The questions that must be dealt with are:

- How can a company monitor and understand rapidly changing customer expectations?
- Which dynamic customer expectations must be met?
- Which ones, if not met, represent real threats to continued business viability?
- Which ones, if performed at industry-best levels, would most impact the bottom line?
- If the company could improve only one thing, what should it be?
- And if it could improve two?
- Three?

Customer value management provides the framework to monitor the marketplace, obtain an actionable customer view, and develop a rational set of business improvement and investment priorities. Fully implemented, CVM methods can prioritize customer needs, wants, and values for action by considering both the customer view (customer-perceived importance and satisfaction levels of needs) and the business view (the impact each expressed need has on buying behavior and the attainment of business goals and objectives).

To secure a customer view of priorities, the customers' vision of ideal value delivery must first be developed, usually by way of focus groups comprised of individual market segments. For example, in Chapter 5 the car rental company learned via focus groups that customers valued assurance of their personal safety while picking up the car. Such specifically identified needs must then be prioritized within the larger list and given relative importance weighting. This is usually accomplished by a subsequent survey to obtain a more statistically representative view from the market segment. The survey secures feedback from a broad base of individual customers on the importance of each of the focus group needs as well as their perception of current performance. By asking the customers how important each need is, not just how well it is performed, the company is able to ensure that questions on surveys are aligned with things that customers think are important. Competitors' customers should also be surveyed to identify gaps between the market's perception of how well the company performs each customer need versus how well key competitors perform.

Competitive performance gaps are a major part of converting the customers' view of priorities to a company view by highlighting the areas of greatest competitive threat to the business. Once the customer view is translated to a company view of business priorities, the CVM framework can be executed to align the firm's capabilities with the customer needs that represent the greatest potential for business improvement. In the case of the car rental company (not Hertz, by the way), the CVM approach revealed that assurance of customers' safety and security was highly important, but it was not provided in a satisfactory manner. The performance of key competitors was also rated significantly higher than that of the company. The combination of focus groups (to identify the need for safety and security) and the quantitative survey (to determine the importance of the need and the relative performance gap with competition) established customer safety as a major business improvement priority. When the firm then looked at the process capabilities and infrastructure to ideally ensure customer safety (e.g. "bring the car to me"), it was evident that major changes were required. Customer value management then defined the specific infrastructure investments the company needed to provide a valet rental car service.

As with many such management disciplines, CVM can be used to develop and implement business priorities with various levels of complexity and sophistication:

- A *bachelor's degree equivalent* might employ relatively standard quantitative market research prioritization techniques to secure customer-defined importance weights and performance perceptions of the individual needs after a CVM customer vision has been identified. This type of a follow on quantitative customer survey establishes de facto business improvement objectives and priorities. For example, this approach identifies needs that customers feel are important, such as safety and security in rental car lots, and helps the company determine the amount of performance improvement required due to low customer satisfaction scores or gaps with competition. However, the specific impact on the business or on buying behavior is not assessed.

- A more complex *master's degree equivalent* might extend the approach by factoring in the Kano framework (Chapter 5) for a more sophisticated analysis. Separating the customer needs into buying-behavior-driver categories allows further analysis of the potential return on investment and helps establish priorities more from the company's point of view. Safety and security, for example, would be identified as a basic must-have need, which if underperformed drives severe dissatisfaction and loss of customers. A Kano-type analysis would identify this type of unmet basic need as a top business improvement opportunity critical to future success.

  In our car rental example, the focus groups envisioned a creative new concept to provide ideal delivery of safety and security: valet rental cars ("bring the car to me"). A master's degree CVM analysis would identify the valet rental car vision as a potential differentiator that could not only stop the current attrition, but could also potentially attract customers away from the competition.

- The *PhD equivalent* might be the use of modeling (e.g., a Dynamic Customer Value Management tool is discussed in Chapter 9): using automation and expert systems to model weighted business priorities based on a combination of customer importance, buying-behavior impacts, and the amount of performance improvement required to close gaps with the competition. Continuing with the car rental company example, this PhD equivalent application of CVM offers the ability to creatively model "what if" scenarios: What if the amount of targeted performance improvement is increased or reduced? What if competitors increased the amount of the performance gap for an individual need, thus increasing the competitive threat and the relative priority weighting for that need? How would business priorities change? How would the priorities for related infrastructure projects change, especially where the infrastructure is linked to several other customer needs?

We introduce examples of each of these approaches to CVM in the remaining chapters of this book. The equivalents to both a bachelor's degree and a master's degree application are discussed in this chapter on prioritization. The PhD level of CVM is discussed in Chapter 9, as we provide an overview of automation to model business improvement scenarios and to optimize management decision making and business design. The choice of methods and techniques will vary depending on the level of sophistication and readiness of a company and the actual business strategy or issues that need to be addressed.

The First Step in Prioritization: All Customers Are Not Equal

The first thing to remember as you begin business prioritization is, as was introduced in Chapter 3, all potential customers are not equal. Some are more desirable than others because they are in segments with greater revenue growth opportunity, higher profit potential, and reduced risk. Or the customers in some segments may simply have needs that match current business capabilities. Market segmentation and targeting are the critical first step to prioritize customer needs for action.

Figure 6-1 depicts the sequence of prioritization that occurs early when executing a CVM framework. The company begins its prioritization when it selects and targets specific customers or segments based on such criteria as their value to the company, their behavior, and/or their compatibility with company strategies or capabilities. And because the behavior of different segments suggests they have different underlying needs, wants, and values, it follows that it potentially costs more or less to attract those different segments. This adds additional variables to customer-prioritization criteria. Industries that are rich in transaction data have an advantage here, as data mining techniques and business intelligence applications convert millions of transactions into clusters of like-behaving customers. When transaction data are coupled with internal and externally acquired databases and customer profiles, customers can be further subsegmented based on current and future profitability, risk assessment, propensity to buy, and other criteria to enable precise targeting (Figure 6-1).

Segmentation: Who Do We Wish to Attract and Retain?

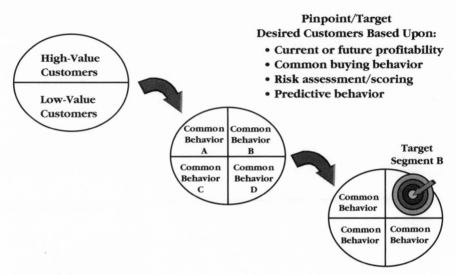

Figure 6-1 Segmentation and targeting: Starting the prioritization process
(© Copyright IBM, 1999)

The Second Step in Prioritization: All Customer Needs Are Not Equal

Once the customers or segments have been prioritized and targeted, their needs must be prioritized. In Chapter 5 we discussed that each of the needs envisioned by a target segment is not of equal weight or importance to that segment. Therefore, the second step in business prioritization is to determine the relative importance to the customers of the needs that are of high value to them. This can be done with varying levels of complexity starting with basic, traditional market research.

Bachelor's Degree CVM

A typical quantitative market research survey determines two things: how important specific customer needs are and how well the customers say a company is providing each of those needs. This type of basic research may be sufficient when a business primarily wants to meet customer expectations and reduce dissatisfaction or attrition. Organizations that are under stress due to high customer dissatisfaction and loss of market share, for example, often only want to quickly understand and improve the few critical things that most account for their defectors.

In this bachelor's degree CVM environment, the company often does not wish to expend the time or resources to become best of breed or invest in a customer vision to provide ideal value. Such a company only wants to identify specific improvement opportunities where customers' minimum expectations are not being met or where gaps exist with competition. What the customer expects becomes the design point for aligning and linking business capabilities and infrastructure to customer needs. Using this approach, the top-ranked needs for business improvement are those that customers indicate are both the most import to them and the most poorly performed.

A problem for more innovative companies that attempt to introduce new and creative delivery of value to increase market share is that typical market research does not link customer needs and importance ratings with buyer decision making. Some customer high-priority needs drive a segment's buying behavior, whereas other professed high-priority needs have little impact on behavior. (Customers may profess to like being greeted at the door of a department store, for example, but may not buy just because someone is there to welcome them.) For those companies, standard approaches fail to answer their most critical issues: Which of these customer needs or product or service attributes would most impact their decision to purchase? Which would increase market share if we were best of breed at delivering? Which can we not afford to invest in because they would not result in a profitable return through increased revenues? For these issues, a more advanced application of CVM is required (Figure 6-2).

Third Step in Prioritization: Moving from a Customer View to a Company View

A major issue in customer-focused business improvement is the translation of the "voice of the customer" to the "voice of the company."

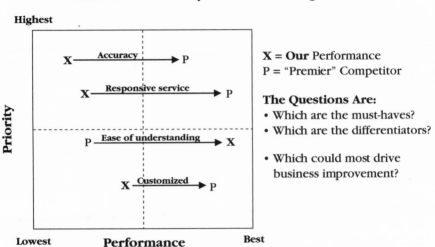

**Standard market research does not answer
"Which two or three of these customer needs
would most drive buyer behavior if improved?"**

Figure 6-2 Standard research: Capturing the customer view of performance
(© Copyright IBM, 1999)

It is important to capture, and then not to lose, the customer view when developing business objectives and priorities. These views, however, must be integrated with the views of the company, which must also consider the needs and interests of its stockholders, its employees, the community, and others such as regulatory agencies or governments. The point is that it is not a simple matter of "let the customers tell us what they want and then give it to them." Significant analyses must be conducted to convert the customer input into business decision-making criteria.

Master's Degree CVM

The bachelor's degree CVM analysis identifies a customer view of needs, wants, and expectations and sets the business objectives and improvement priorities accordingly. A more investment-oriented master's CVM analysis is possible to move from a customer view to a company view by linking customer needs to their buying behavior and bottom-line results. At this level, a combination of more sophisticated techniques may be employed by adding advanced CVM approaches to the standard research, such as:

- Focus groups to develop a vision by customers of creative, new, added value at key interactions that could differentiate the firm and make it their preferred provider. Such an ideal-value vision effectively moves the design point for business improvement away from "meet customer expectations" to "establish and fulfill new value propositions that exceed expectations."

- Subsequent quantitative surveys, including a Kano-like analysis, to identify the actual buying behavior that the envisioned needs and wants would generate and the level of company performance or investment required to generate it.

The potential for this company-view dimension of prioritization was introduced in Chapter 5 with the Kano framework, which stated that customer needs are not all equal in importance in the minds of the customers and, more important, do not have an equal impact upon a business (Figure 6-3).

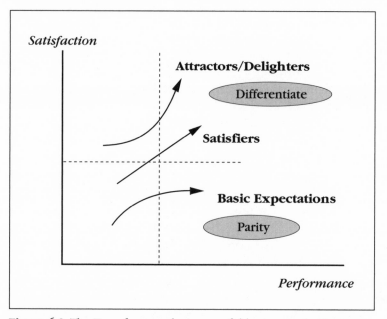

Figure 6-3 The Kano framework: A powerful business prioritization tool (Adapted from work by Dr. N. Kano, Science University of Tokyo)

Dr. Kano's findings provide a basis to prioritize customer needs and wants from a new perspective: the impact on buyer behavior and bottom-line business results. Our coverage of the needs hierarchy in Chapter 5 focused on how Dr. Kano's work segments customer needs into a hierarchy that links to their behavior. It was this concept of a customer-needs hierarchy that allowed IBM to move ahead on several key business processes and to develop new, innovative reengineering approaches. By adapting the Kano framework as input to business reengineering, IBM was able to take a huge list of customer needs and wants and rationalize them into investment priorities, each with a different potential business impact. IBM also determined that it is all right to have heroic performance objectives for all company employees; however, you do not want to invest equally to attain them or have the same performance level (e.g., zero defects) for all objectives. It is not appropriate or cost effective. You do not want to be world-class at all things.

When coupled with CVM approaches, the Kano framework becomes a powerful business tool for prioritizing customer needs and for pinpointing business investments. For example, when customer needs are placed into Kano's three categories, each category represents major business prioritization criteria:

- *Basic needs,* the bottom category on the Kano framework (Figure 6-3), are the basic building blocks or cornerstone requirements to be in business. They represent the needs with the greatest potential negative impact on a business. Basic needs, such as answering the phone or having a safe and reliable system to deliver goods and services, must be provided or customers will leave. An important observation by Dr. Kano is that basic needs are a one-way phenomenon. As cited at the beginning of this chapter, doing the basics poorly will drive customers away. Doing them extremely well, however (arriving for meetings early or answering the phone in one ring, to name a few examples), will not drive ever-higher satisfaction, nor will it lure competitors' customers to switch their loyalties to you. The implications of this are that the relative impact and prioritization criteria for basic needs should be based only on preventing underperformance: Not providing them will result in business failure. This invaluable insight can be used both to ensure that minimum needs are met and to prevent unnecessary investment in overperformance of those same basic needs.

From a company viewpoint, then, and utilizing a master's degree CVM analysis, unmet basic expectations are the highest priority or tier of customer needs for business improvement. Customers will defect if these are performed poorly. Examples of such top priorities include:

1. Basic must-have needs, which are underperformed versus customers' specific minimum expectations.

2. Basic must-have needs, where no specific minimum standard is known, but which are performed below the industry average of all successful competitors (the industry average performance level becomes the de facto standard, as you do not need to become best of breed at these basic needs).

- *Satisfier needs* are the middle category on the Kano framework (Figure 6-3), but the least important to the company. These do not individually drive customer buying behavior. (For example, a sparkling clean service department or leather chairs in automobile dealership waiting rooms may receive high satisfaction on an opinion survey, but they have little or no impact on the customer's decision regarding the next car purchased.)

The satisfier category represents the needs that exceed minimum basic expectations and put smiles on the faces of customers and improve satisfaction surveys. But since they do not (as a single or individual need) drive buying behavior, they are individually a lower priority for business improvement than unmet basic needs or attractors. Collectively, if affordable, a group of them may add to a business or brand image and warrant investment.

From a company viewpoint, the individual satisfiers become the lowest, or bottom priority, for business improvement consideration.

- *Attractor needs,* the top category on the Kano framework graphic (Figure 6-3), are the needs which, if performed best in the industry, deliver such value to the customer that they can differentiate the company and attract market share from competitors. Corporate customers, for example, can often experience significant cost reduction to their own processes if supplier processes are ideally designed to interface. A customer that conducts millions of transactions could enjoy significant cost reduction from a supplier whose invoices are easy to process. The implications of attractors are that "the party who performs best wins." These are the customer needs that the CEO of the financial services company had in mind when he said, "I only want to be the best at the critical few things that will have a direct effect on my bottom line!"

From a company viewpoint, once the minimum basic needs are met, attractor needs then represent the next highest priority, with the greatest potential for business improvement. Customers will be attracted by the firm that performs these best. Examples of this important group include:

1. Attractor needs that are currently being underperformed by the company and lag industry-best competition. For example, home delivery and shelf stocking of groceries are now offered for a very minimal fee in some areas of the Northeast. This is an attractor for huge segments of affluent singles and for couples with busy schedules. As the premium charge for this service goes down (and it will), the value will go up, further differentiating the provider. This will place intense pressure on traditional grocery stores to close that value gap to remain in business.

2. Attractor needs that are not provided today by any company within the industry, but that are becoming technologically possible. For example, the Internet now offers an unprecedented vehicle for firms to identify creative new forms of delivering customer value. Digital publishing of books, music, and videos and the efficient distribution of them worldwide were not a technical possibility until the Internet became a commercial reality. Firms in all industries are now looking at the Internet as a new potential element in their infrastructure. By working the CVM pyramid backward (from bottom to top), they are considering the new capabilities that this infrastructure could enable and, in turn, the possibilities for new, creative delivery of customer value.

Such a Kano-like master's application of CVM classifies customer needs according to the company or business view of potential benefits. The customer view is maintained, however, via ongoing surveys of each customer segment to monitor their specific needs hierarchy and priorities. For example: Which of these needs, if provided exceptionally well by a new supplier, could attract you to change vendors? And for these vendor-differentiating needs, please indicate their relative importance to you on a scale of 1–10.

Note: Customers do not always know and will not always tell you the exact impact of a need on their behavior. This can often be statistically derived once the firm has implemented a process or service by correlating the customer satisfaction measurements of each need with actual subsequent transactions and purchase behavior. In the case of CVM, however, we often deal with a perspective that does not yet exist. In such cases, the buying behavior impact of an unimplemented vision cannot be measured or analyzed. Customers can only be surveyed and directly asked to anticipate the future buying behavior that each element of their vision would generate and the relative importance of each need.

A master's CVM customer view not only helps establish business improvement priorities, but it also defines which competitors should become the company's benchmark for performance comparisons. For basic needs, the company should compare itself to the average performance level for its industry (the de facto standard, as the company does not want to be the best). For attractors, the benchmark and performance standard should be the best-of-breed competitor (any performance less than the best exposes the firm to lost customers). Minimal energy should be expended regarding benchmark research on satisfiers. However, if several satisfiers appear to have the potential to collectively attract customers when provided as a group (e.g., if they could be combined and implemented together at a sufficiently low cost), these should be benchmarked and compared against the industry average performance and low-cost providers.

GTE Wireless: Behavior-Driver Categories for Internal I/T Customers. When GTE Wireless used CVM to identify the needs of the internal customers of its I/T organization, the company found that the standard nomenclature for the three behavior categories of customer needs did not apply. Internal customers do not typically use outside vendors, so business prioritization criteria could not be based on which needs would make them leave if not provided or which needs would attract them from competitors if performed well. GTE wireless elected to continue to use the CVM three-tier approach to develop a rational prioritization scheme, but found that they must rename the categories to apply to three types of impact on their own business. Since the customers were internal GTE customers of I/T processes, the criteria were renamed to reflect their individual impact on the bottom-line of GTE's business:

- Basic needs were defined as critical internal customer needs that, if not met, would seriously impair that business unit's overall operational effectiveness. Failure to meet a basic need would create significant customer dissatisfaction and could result in lost opportunity for additional business (i.e., lost market share for GTE).

- Satisfier needs were defined as expressed needs that were neither a basic nor an attractor need.

- Attractor/differentiator needs were defined as those critical few that, if performed exceptionally well, would do more than put a smile on the internal customer's face. They would significantly enhance the business unit's bottom-line profitability. Meeting attractor needs would result in delighted internal and external customers and an increased desire to do business (i.e., additional market share for GTE).

GTE Wireless took the ÇVM concepts and modified them to fit their internal environment and to reflect the impacts on the business of meeting (or not meeting) the requests of internal customers.

Gwinnett County Schools: Behavior-Driver Categories for Nonbusiness Environments. Customer relationships often occur in contexts other than a business environment, such as when the customer is the recipient of a product or service from a nonprofit or government agency. Customer value management approaches continue to apply in these instances, but the terminology may need to be changed. A creative application of CVM to align a nonbusiness organization's I/T strategy with the needs of its customers occurred at Gwinnett County Public Schools in Atlanta, GA. The primary product or service provided by the school district is education. The school district comprises a value chain of staff and teachers who collectively fulfill the needs of an ultimate end customer, the student. As members of the value chain, the teachers and administrators are customers of the school district's I/T organization, and they are also suppliers of the end product to the student. When analyzing a value chain for internal customers' needs, CVM encourages the use of the external customer as the focus and design point. Gwinnett Schools easily adopted this approach to prioritization and defined their three tiers of customer needs as:

- Basic needs, or things that are required for the teaching and learning process to occur. Their absence has a direct and negative effect on student learning.
- Satisfiers, or things that affect the productivity and/or job satisfaction of teachers, other staff, and administrators but have only an indirect effect on student learning.
- Delighters, or things that have a significant, highly positive impact on student learning the more they are provided.

To develop their vision, including quantification and prioritization of customer needs, Gwinnett utilized focus groups with teachers and administrators to generate their hypotheses regarding needs and the appropriate priority tier. Subsequent quantitative surveys were conducted with over 2000 students and parents to validate and quantify the requirements. These were used to distill a lengthy list down to the top needs, which became the design points for the district's strategic technology plan and the focus for new management initiatives and projects.

Using Customer Value Management: Prioritization Scenarios

When choosing and applying the appropriate CVM methods for prioritization, there are four major variables to consider (Figure 6-4). These fall into two categories: scope and approach:

1. The scope of the issue to be addressed
   - *Design a totally new process or service.* The prioritization of customer needs for a new process considers only the importance of the needs. The most important needs become top design priorities; they must all be included in the new process, irrespective of how well they are being performed in the old one.

- *Design improvements to an existing process or service.* The prioritization of customer needs for process improvement considers both the importance and the current performance of each
  customer need in the existing process. Only the most important
  needs, which are also the most poorly performed, become the
  top improvement priorities.

2. The CVM approach to be used
   - *Bachelor's CVM,* when the analysis will focus only on the voice
     of the customer (customer-perceived importance or perfor-
     mance of each need).
   - *Master's CVM,* when the analysis will also include the voice of
     the company (customer view, plus a business view of buyer
     behavior impacts).

Examples follow of the two business scopes (a new process or
service and improvements to an existing one) and of utilizing each
of the two CVM approaches to address these issues. In some cases,
the business may want to expend only a minimal amount of energy
or investment, and the issue may only warrant a short-form (bachelor's) CVM approach. In others, a more sophisticated (master's)

Customer Needs: Prioritization/Weighting

		Bachelor's CVM (Customer view)	Master's CVM (Company view)
		Approach	
1. Design a new process	*S c o*	• Customers' importance weights	• Customers' importance weights • Plus additional percent based on the (Kano category) business impact
2. Improve an existing process	*p e*	• Customers' importance weights • Plus current performance gaps Additional percent weighting based on performance improvement required to close gaps	• Customers' importance weights • Plus current performance gaps Additional percent weighting based on performance improve-ment required to close gaps • Plus additional percent based on the (Kano category) business impact

Figure 6-4 Applying the concepts: New process versus improve existing (bache-lor's versus master's) (© Copyright IBM, 1999)

application of the methods may be required when significant long-term investments are being made or critical customer relationships are at stake.

Prioritzation for a New Process or Service

A New Process or Service: Bachelor's CVM

To prioritize customer needs for a new process or service, using a standard bachelor's CVM approach, all of the customers' most important needs should be considered top priorities for the new process. Customer responses to quantitative survey questions (e.g., How important are each of the following needs on a scale of 1–10?) establish the customer-defined priorities for a new process design (Figure 6-5).

Figure 6-5 depicts a hypothetical situation wherein customers have identified six things they expect from a business process such as customer service. When asked to indicate the relative importance of these items, the customers indicated that each of the needs has the exact same level of importance. Note: For our example, each need is weighted as 10 on a scale of 1 (not very important) to 10 (critically important). While this might never happen in an actual business situation, this will allow us to demonstrate later the relative power of adding additional CVM data to enable management decision making.

Here we have only the customer view of the relative importance of each need. If a new or significantly reengineered process or service is required, all of the most important needs are usually considered to be the design requirements and are the business priorities based on this limited type of data.

A New Process or Service: Master's CVM

However, with a master's level of CVM, one has the capability to add additional (Kano-like) buying behavior information to the importance weightings, effectively changing the weights to reflect the company's

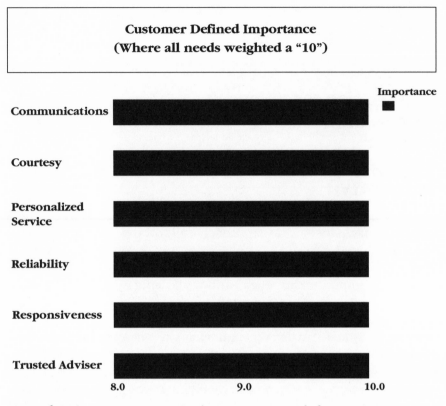

Figure 6-5 The customer view: Weighting customer needs for a new process or service

view of importance (Figure 6-6). Whereas in Figure 6-5 all the needs were originally weighted by customers as a 10, the following master's example depicts the company viewpoint by multiplying those weights by an additional factor that represents each item's buying-behavior-driver (Kano) category. In the case of basic needs, the company recognizes the additional importance to the business of meeting basic needs by multiplying/uplifting the customer's importance weights by an additional 1.5 (i.e., 10 × 1.5 = 15). This effectively uplifts the weight of all basic needs as a group by 50 percent and insures that they become the top tier of company business priorities (Figure 6-6).

For the attractor needs, the customer-defined importance weights are multiplied by 1.2 (i.e., 10 × 1.2 = 12), which effectively groups

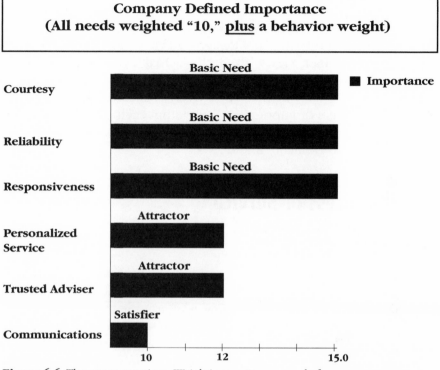

Figure 6-6 The company view: Weighting customer needs for a new process or service

and elevates them by 20 percent to become a second tier of business priorities. (Remember, the basic needs must first be met before a business can differentiate itself by investments in these attractor needs.)

The satisfier needs are not uplifted (i.e., 10 × 1.0 = 10). They remain with their original customer weightings as the bottom-most grouping of business priorities.

This results in three sets of priority tiers, each of which contains an array of prioritized needs within the tier, but each tier has a significantly different business impact. The tiers represent a company view of the impacts of the customer needs. Figure 6-6 demonstrates the additional "decision-making granularity" that can be obtained from including buyer behavior in the analyses and also how it dramatically "breaks out of the pack" the most important needs and keeps them in groups. In the figure, it is clear that some customer needs have significantly greater impact on the business and that the different effects of each of the three groups of needs must be considered when setting business investment priorities.

Note: Had the customers not designated each need as 10 in importance (the customer view), then the actual designated customer importance weight of each need would have been multiplied in the example by 1.5, 1.2, or 1.0, respectively, still breaking them into three separate tiers of importance. But within each Kano tier, the relative weights and sequence-in-importance of needs assigned by the customers would be maintained.

A New Process or Service versus Improvement of an Existing One

The foregoing examples depict alternate methods to prioritize customer needs when designing a new business or new process or service (or when one performs so poorly that a totally new one must be engineered or reengineered). When such a new process or service is required, the existing performance or delivery level of each customer need is irrelevant. All of the most important needs must be included in the new design, irrespective of their current performance. However, in the following scenarios, management must prioritize incremental improvements to portions of an existing process or service, not design and engineer a fundamentally new one. For incremental improvement of an existing process, the business-prioritization criteria must consider both the importance weight of each need (as defined earlier) and the current performance level. The top business improvement priorities would be the needs that are both most important and most poorly performed. For a more robust prioritization, the performance of key competitors must also be considered to better understand the degree of improvement effort that will be required to meet or exceed the competition.

Improve an Existing Process or Service: Bachelor's CVM

From the customers' viewpoint, the improvement priorities for a specific company are a function of both how important an item is and how well it is currently performed by the company. This improvement priority may be computed and graphically depicted by a combined weight that reflects both the customer-defined importance of each need and their perception of the amount of improvement required. When a company significantly lags the competition in delivery of a need, the potential to improve the business by a focus on this item is much greater than for a company that already performs ahead of the competition. To reflect this difference, a CVM practitioner will uplift the customers' importance weights to reflect the additional emphasis that the particular company must place on the item due to its underperformance (Figure 6-7).

In Figure 6-7 the customer view of improvement priorities is depicted by a relative 10 percent additional uplift in importance of the three needs (communications, personalized service, responsiveness) that the customers believe are currently underperformed

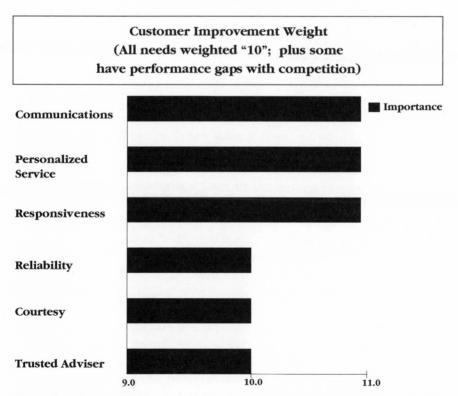

Figure 6-7 The customer view: Weighting customer needs to reflect improvement priority

and lagging competitive performance by 10 percent. In our original "new process" scenario (Figure 6-5), each of the six needs had importance weights of 10. That would also be their importance in a "process improvement" scenario if they were all performed satisfactorily or not lagging the competition. In our process improvement example, however, the customers perceive the company to be underperforming three needs by 10 percent (i.e., when they compare the company's performance to the competition, or when customer satisfaction is 9 on a scale of 10). An additional 10 percent is added to the importance weightings for those three items to reflect the customers' view that this company needs 10 percent more focus and performance improvement on them. From the customers' view, the degree of underperformance (i.e., when compared to the competition) of a need makes it that (degree) much more important to be improved than other similar needs. The graphic depicts their view.

Improve an Existing Process or Service: Master's CVM

For a more precise level of detail, the CVM practitioner can add an additional factor: the relative behavior impact of each need on buyers and the potential for subsequent business improvement. This provides a significantly more granular and detailed analysis for management prioritization and decision making (Figure 6-8).

Figure 6-8 captures the power of fully applied CVM methods and techniques. Master's methods in this final example use importance weights, behavior categories, and performance gaps to identify a highly granular set of business improvement priorities. The customer needs in Figure 6-5 were all weighted as a 10, which had relatively little value to management for prioritization. But by applying additional CVM methods, this becomes (Figure 6-8) a more detailed and actionable analysis with five levels of priorities for focused business investments. In this process improvement scenario, basic needs that do not underperform specific customer expectations or lag the average competitor, such as "courtesy" and "reliability" (Figure 6-7), are not extraordinary opportunities for improvement, so they are not uplifted by a factor of 1.5 as they would be in a new process design scenario. Such satisfactorily performed basic needs

Figure 6-8 The company view: Weighting customer needs to reflect improvement priority

tend to drop to the bottom of a master's level process improvement analysis (Figure 6-8). However, a basic need that is a dissatisfier or that lags the average competitor, such as "responsiveness" in Figure 6-7, represents a major opportunity for this company to improve its business and is uplifted and weighted accordingly in Figure 6-8. The second most important category for business improvement is comprised of differentiaters, such as "personalized service" in Figure 6-7, and its master's CVM weighting in Figure 6-8 includes additional emphasis required to close a 10 percent performance gap with the best competitor.

A company's market research will identify a range of importance weights for the needs, and not all will be rated the same, as in our original example (Figure 6-5). Some of the needs may be weighted the same, but others will be weighted by customers across a wide array of importance metrics. The company that applies CVM methods, however, will find that this customer view can be expanded into a company view for business investments where:

- Needs that appear to be weighted relatively similar to others in the customer view can become very different, and much more granular, company priorities.

- Needs that appear to be weighted relatively lower than others in the customer view can become part of a much higher tier of business priorities. Negative performance gaps with competition can further increase their importance as an opportunity for additional investment.

- Needs that appear to be weighted higher than others in the customer view can become part of a much lower tier of business priorities. Positive performance gaps with competition can further reduce their importance as a focus area for additional investment.

PhD CVM

With the additional application of automation and other disciplines, such as modeling of alternative scenarios, it is possible to practice these approaches at an even higher level of sophistication and precision. Quantitative market research data and Dynamic CVM automated applications can enable a company to monitor the customer view as part of an ongoing business process to identify changing customer needs and align business investment priorities. The outputs of these automated approaches may be fed into a management system that is actually driven by the customer view. These concepts are discussed further in Chapter 9.

Summary of CVM Prioritization Approaches

Management faces a rapidly changing field of play in which all customers are not equal in their importance to a business and all customer needs do not have an equal effect on buying behavior. Prioritization of customer needs must include targeting the customers as well as their needs based on many factors, most of which are in a constant state of flux. Typical market research approaches are no longer sufficient in this environment. Today, a combination of business intelligence or data mining (to segment and target customers), qualitative research (to envision changing ideal value propositions), and quantitative research on customer needs (to identify importance weights, performance gaps and behavior impacts) is required. The company's intent (new or improved processes, meet minimum needs or attract additional market share) will determine which methods or approaches should be used. It is important to use the correct approach based on the business situation and the desired results. The outputs of the analysis can be dramatically different depending on which technique is appropriate and applied, as demonstrated in Figures 6-5 through 6-8.

In Figure 6-6, although all the needs were initially weighted 10 by the customer, the CVM approach identifies those that are must-haves and that must be included in a new process design. The remaining needs, by definition, are not must-haves and are highlighted as optional requirements for further financial analysis. Adding this behavior-driver viewpoint to the analysis results in a different set of "top" investment priorities, no longer weighted the same, that are more aligned with the interests of the firm.

In Figure 6-7 the business issue is to improve an existing process. An additional weighting factor is added to represent the amount of process performance improvement necessary for each customer need. This incorporates the relative size of performance gaps with competition into the prioritization. The customer needs that lag the competition with the largest performance gaps receive relatively greater business priority and weighting. Again, a new set of priorities is derived focusing the company's need to improve only portions of an existing process.

And in Figure 6-8 the master's level CVM approach carves the six customer needs into five significantly more actionable improvement priorities from the company's perspective. This is accomplished by combining and analyzing each need's relative customer importance weighting, buyer-behavior impact, and amount of performance gap with competition. Customer value management approaches in this figure generate five levels of granularity and ranking/weighting of the needs to pinpoint decision making.

Whichever approach is used (Figures 6-5 through 6-8), CVM enables management to transform an undisciplined menu of customer needs into a prioritized set of customer requirements for business investments. The next step, discussed in Chapter 7, is to complete the company view by identifying the required business capabilities and their relative cost to implement.

EXERCISE
Applying CVM to Your Business

Management Issues

How do you prioritize your customers' needs as opportunities for investment? What are the impacts of different customer needs and wants on your business strategy? Which dynamic customer needs must be met? Which, if not met, represent a threat to continued business viability? Which ones, if performed at industry-best levels, would most impact the bottom line?

1. Commodity provider
   - Is your strategy to compete on price?
   - Which customer needs should be eliminated from your process or service designs to reduce costs but without losing customers?
   - Which customer needs must be met, and the costs must be included in your process designs? For these, what is the gap between your performance and your customers' expectations and requirements? What is the gap between your performance and that of your key competitors?
   - Which needs should be eliminated from satisfaction surveys because they do not impact buyer behavior and are therefore irrelevant?
   - If you could improve only one thing, what should it be? If you could improve two? Three?

2. Added-value provider
   - Is your strategy to compete on value?
   - Which basic must-have needs are weighted the highest by customers and have the largest performance gaps versus expected performance or with average competition?
   - Which attractor, differentiating needs are weighted the highest by high-profit customers? Which needs are not provided by the industry? Or which needs have significant performance gaps between your company and the industry-best competitor?

continued

- Which needs should be eliminated from satisfaction surveys and investment priorities because they are irrelevant to business performance?
- If you could improve performance or delivery of one customer need, which one would it be? If you could improve two? Three?

7

Design

Envisioning "Ideal" Customer-Defined Business Capabilities

Charlie, I could've been a contender.
MARLON BRANDO, ON THE WATERFRONT

Business improvement tools du jour over the past few years have included total quality management (TQM), continuous process improvement (CPI), business process management (BPM), benchmarking, downsizing, reengineering for cost efficiency, and many others intended to make the organization a contender in the marketplace. Most recently, the search for a management Holy Grail has shifted to become close to the customer. The following excerpt is from a series of management briefings entitled "Close to the Customer," recently copublished with Professor Merlin Stone of the Surrey European School of Management.

> MBNA, a loan and credit card company, reduced its defection rate from 10% to 5% per annum and increased its profits by 85%. It did so not by introducing a loyalty scheme, but by completely overhauling its service delivery system via business process re-engineering techniques. This means that it *redesigned its systems and processes for managing customers to meet customers' requirements* rather than the functional requirements of different departments. Service quality went up, defections went down and profits soared.[1]

[1]Merlin Stone, Harvey Thompson, and Derek Davies, "Customer Loyalty and Continuity: The Acquisition, Development and Retention of Profitable Customers," in *Close to the Customer,* pp. 12–13. Bedford, England: Policy Publications, Ltd.

This passage from one of our briefings relates to the search by management for ways to attract and retain customers effectively. Loyalty programs such as grocery stores rewarding frequent shoppers with air miles redeemable for travel are an example of the current proliferation of such schemes. At the end of the day, however, the contenders for high profit and customer loyalty will be companies that are willing to make fundamental changes in their infrastructure and process capabilities to align themselves with the needs of the customer. Firms that elect to go only with the loyalty scheme of the day may end up like Terry Malloy, the ex-pug turned longshoreman played by Marlon Brando in the classic film, *On the Waterfront,* a might-have-been who missed his chance to be a winner.

The CVM pyramid is a vehicle to help align the business with the customer. The alignment is executed top-down, unlike the pyramids constructed in ancient Egypt or at prehistoric Chichén Itzá, which as far as we know were constructed from the bottom up (Figure 7-1).

The Customer View

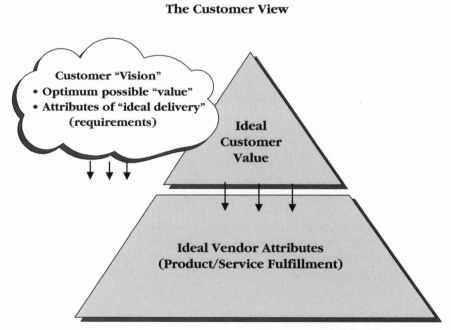

Figure 7-1 The top of the pyramid: The customer view (© Copyright IBM, 1999)

A customer-centered enterprise literally starts with the customers' viewpoint and then determines what the business must be good at doing (capabilities) and what things must be physically present to have those capabilities (infrastructure). To make that relationship graphically clear, CVM places the customer view at the top, or apex, of a business blueprint or pyramid. Once the customers' vision is identified and business priorities are established to invest in a new design, or to improve an existing one, the focus shifts toward the base of the CVM pyramid. The business capabilities and required infrastructure are then designed to support and fulfill the customers' vision (Figure 7-2).

Each customer need identified as a high-priority is analyzed to identify the specific required capabilities and enabling infrastructure. As the analysis progresses, the highest leverage infrastructure elements (those that enable multiple capabilities and multiple customer needs) will become apparent.

The following examples will help illustrate the concepts. Our experience with the customers of major automotive, petrochemical, financial services, manufacturing, telecommunications,

The Company View

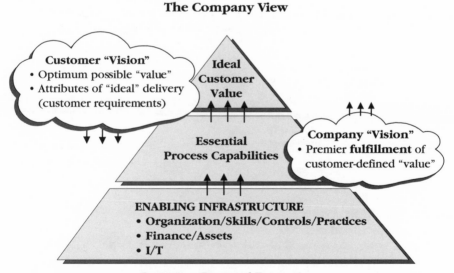

Customer-Centered Enterprise

Figure 7-2 The bottom of the pyramid: The company view (© Copyright IBM, 1999)

retail, distribution, utilities, and information technologies companies has shown these to be representative customer needs. Yet, most companies have a marked absence of the business capabilities and infrastructure required to meet these needs effectively, as well as other (less generic) critical requirements identified by their customers.

The first example, customized service delivery, is fast becoming a universal chorus from customers as they become accustomed to personalized treatment from high-service industries. Today, the customer vision increasingly is to have things "my way" (Figure 7-3). For the company, the issue is to identify exactly what that means in terms of:

- New business capabilities: What actions must the customer-facing business processes be able to do? How much process flexibility is required? How can that flexibility be provided at affordable cost?

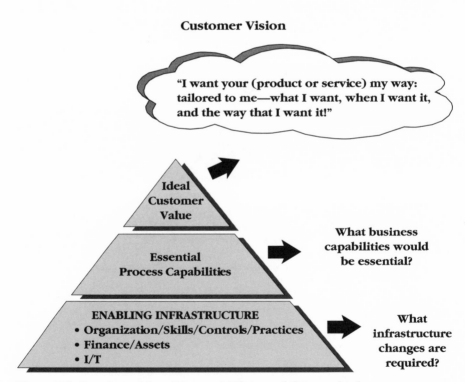

Figure 7-3 Customer vision: "My way." What capabilities and infrastructure are required? (© Copyright IBM, 1999)

What back-office support processes must be aligned? What information must both customer-facing and support processes be able (capable) to access?

- Infrastructure investments: What organization or specialized skills are required? What management systems and controls are needed? What procedures and documentation would institutionalize and standardize the methods? What measurements would be required? How will new employee behavior be incented and rewarded? What policies or practices will be needed? What information and technology will be necessary?

For example, what must a company do to meet the customers' need for personalized invoices? How can the company ensure the delivery of this customer-defined outcome? The following are some of the things a business might require to provide such a service. This is not a complete list; it is intended only to illustrate how the CVM pyramid framework is used to identify specific actions for a company to meet a specific customer need, such as to provide invoices, "my way."

The pyramid for this example has three sections.

1. Customer needs. This is a customer-defined vision of both basic expectations and ideal value delivery at each interaction with the business enterprise, or with a specific process under analysis. These are usually expressed as outcomes from the interaction, such as "quick access to information," "easy to understand," or as the example in Figure 7-3 illustrates, a personalized service tailored to the customer "my way."

2. Process capabilities. These are the few critical things that must be done and which the business or process must be capable of doing well in order to deliver against each of the customer needs. To be capable of providing tailored, personalized service delivery, a company's invoicing process must be able to:

- *Capture and retain exactly how each customer wants his or her invoice.* While some customers typically want only a single invoice, others desire certain items to be grouped and billed on separate invoices, and still others want even different forms of customization such as quarterly invoices, special handling and routing, or custom formatting to make them easier to administer for payment. For efficiency, the business capability to capture and retain these customer preferences should reside in other upstream processes, where customer interactions occur earlier than billing, such as during the sales or order fulfillment processes. This allows one-time data capture at the front end of a relationship for later use by downstream processes and customer-support activities.

- *Access each individual customer's preferences at the time of service delivery.* The information regarding a customer's preferences often resides in a database or customer profile; however, access to that information must be distributed to all of the support processes and personnel that subsequently deal with the customer. Full information regarding customers can then be accessed, just in time, during service delivery. The invoicing process in a customer-centered company, for example, has the capability to access information regarding each customer's billing preferences while the process is being executed.

- *Provide the invoice in different ways.* To provide a service "my way" to a customer in an efficient and effective manner, the company must also understand how their customers cluster into groups with common needs. Modular processes can then be designed with several different capability modules that match the needs of different customer segments. The business is then able to offer a range of alternatives to customers, which provide to each customer the appearance of receiving a tailored and personalized service. However, the company is actually capable of mass producing the service (in this case, invoices) for a large cost-effective group, or segment, of people who happen to want invoices the same way (mass customization). Modular capabilities that can be "snapped together" just in time provide customer-centered companies with an ability to do their customer-facing or support processes many different ways, including the way that many individual customers desire.

- *Use the customer's preference data to drive the actual service delivery.* The invoicing process must then be able to systematically engage the correct service delivery process capability module just in time (e.g., grouping the customer's items, as desired, onto different invoices) based on each customer's preference data.

And here is an example of how several business capabilities must link and align: The three prior capabilities must be present in order to have this fourth one, and collectively, they ensure the delivery of what the customer values (CVM).

3. Enabling infrastructure. These are the physical things (dependencies or prerequisites) that must be present in the infrastructure to support (enable) the essential process capabilities. There is no one way to enable a business capability; however, to provide personalized invoice delivery, the business infrastructure items might include:

- *Organization.* Organizational alignment is a powerful enabler of specific business capabilities. Specialization, for example, groups required functional skills into a common organizational structure for better management focus and control. Customer value management methods identify the organizational enablers that align and link to specific capabilities required to meet target customer needs. In the case of personalized invoicing ("my way"):

  A billing, invoicing, or customer service functional department ensures a concentration of skills to enable execution of such a complex business process.

  A business process center of competency is an organizational enabler to assist the functional departments, such as billing, invoicing, or customer service, to manage and improve the flow and execution of their horizontal processes.

- *Management and measurement systems.* Business process management disciplines, such as standardized, documented, repeatable, and predictable administrative processes, enable execution of the complex capabilities (in this case, invoicing) required to meet customer needs in the same way, every time. This can be provided via detailed manual process flows and desk procedures or by automated "smart processes" which contain embedded process knowledge and walk the employee through the critical path. Process-centric measurements ensure that the manual desk procedures are performed correctly, while the automated processes contain self-edits and controls that audit, manage, and enforce critical path activities and process execution.

- *Customer satisfaction surveys and formalized feedback.* In CVM, the customer is the design point for business capabilities and is at both the start and the finish of process design and execution. Customer requirements begin the design (and the later execution) of each customer-facing or support process. After the process is executed and a product or service is delivered, the customer becomes the final arbiter as to whether or not the transaction was successfully completed. Posttransaction customer surveys provide a major source of feedback, which in turn becomes a critical input to enable continuous business improvement.

- *Employee objectives and incentives.* When IBM began to implement business process management, the company initially experienced limited business results. The processes were redesigned, but the company culture and employee behavior were not. They remained functionally oriented. However, when the employees were positioned within a context of being constituents inside of a process, and when their personal objectives and incentives were tied to their execution of the process and to subsequent customer satisfaction, things changed. Processes became increasingly dominant within the company, and customer satisfaction became a primary driver of behavior.

- *Skills and training.* Employees trained on process procedure enable consistent execution of a standardized process. Education on how to access customer-preference information and to input that into the invoicing process, for example, enables the capability to provide that service "my way."

- *Customer-focused policies and practices.* A customer-first policy sets the tone and standard for employees. This ensures that employees understand a hierarchy of decision-making criteria when dealing with customers and which of these criteria are most important. At Disney World, for example, employees have a hierarchy of company values (policies) that they use to make good decisions on the job. Disney employees are trained to think of themselves as constantly on stage and that the theme park is an ongoing "show" for their guests. When Disney employees step behind the "employee only" doorways, they are literally offstage. They therefore understand the value that is placed on a good show. However, the hierarchy of several values that employees are taught begins: safety, then show, and so on. This tells the employee that when an elderly person is entering or exiting a ride, safety comes first, so it is okay to stop the ride, even if that interferes with the show. Such clearly articulated policies and practices are a powerful means to drive consistent behavior and attain a desired company culture.

- *Business strategy and practices to target key customer segments.* A customer-centered business vision, mission, and strategy put clarity around whom the company's products and services must satisfy. Formal methods (data mining, marketing research, CVM) to cluster and then target individual customers who have common needs or preferences make the strategy actionable and generate investments in capabilities that align with each segment.

- *Business practice to capture individual customer preferences.* Standardized practices and procedures ensure that critical customer data, such as their invoice preferences, are documented as part of the formal enrollment or registration of new customers and updated at appropriate subsequent interactions.

- *Information and information technology.* A database and profiling applications provide the means to record individual customer preferences when an account is opened. Real-time access by customer-facing employees to view the data, possibly via an on-line network, enables highly personalized service. Additionally, smart processes with automated applications ensure consistent, predictable outcomes, such as invoices "my way" (e.g., programs that utilize customer-needs data to assemble the correct process steps or modules for an individual service transaction).

This analysis, while not complete, illustrates how a company can take one customer-desired outcome, or attribute of a process or service, and convert that into business requirements. As basic as many customer needs may sound, businesses do not normally monitor and maintain an ongoing alignment between the infrastructure that supports each customer interaction and the associated customer view. As a result, especially during times of great change, the business may drift apart from the customer without management awareness.

Often, it is the most basic of needs that the company is unable to fulfill. For example, "meet your commitments" is something virtually every customer expects, and which one would assume every major company could ensure. However, many companies fail to institutionalize and enforce standard processes that ensure consistent employee performance. And even corporations with thick procedure manuals (and tens of thousands of employees in daily contact with customers) find this basic business requirement extremely difficult to achieve. (How many times have you not had a phone call returned within 24 hours or a service provided as promised?) The CVM framework provides a simple format to analyze what must be done to achieve such a critical must-have customer need (Figure 7-4).

Consider the customer value pyramid in Figure 7-4. If customers expect you to meet your commitments consistently, what must you be capable of doing well and what must be present to enable those capabilities? Using CVM and working backward from the desired outcome (meet your commitments), the company must first be able to make a valid commitment and then be able to meet it.

1. Process capabilities. To both make and meet commitments consistently, a business must be able to:

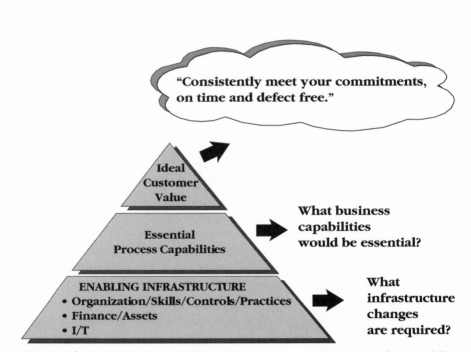

Figure 7-4 Customer vision: "Make and meet your commitments." What capabilities and infrastructure are required? (© Copyright IBM, 1999)

- *Understand the customer request.* From the customer's perspective, the business must be able to understand what the customer wants (and often further understand what they actually need) based on insights into the customer and the customer's request.

- *Understand the company products, services, and processes.* Customer-contact personnel must have an analytical understanding of their own company products, services, processes, contract terms, and conditions. They also need the ability to ensure that different potential configurations or combinations will work together.

- *Develop a valid commitment (a "deal").* A valid commitment requires an ability to determine which of the company's product or service options apply to the customer's request. Customer-contact personnel must be able to identify the critical path of activities that are needed and then predict how long the committed action will take. They must also understand the company's delivery capabilities as well as those of third parties in the supply chain, such as production lead times and available inventory.

- *Make a valid commitment.* To make a commitment requires the capability to commit actions by others, such as subsequent activities by service personnel or by the manufacturing and distribution functions, to meet a product delivery date. This often includes multiple cross-functional organizations and can involve a series of internal functions, business partners, and other third parties.

- *Capture and retain commitments.* The ability of a business process or of extended-enterprise value chain participants to execute a high volume of commitments consistently depends on a capability to methodically capture and then access a history of commitments or deals in process.

- *Communicate commitments cross-functionally.* The members of the value chain (i.e., cross-functional manufacturing or service personnel) must be identified and advised of all commitments made to customers that require their attention.

- *Monitor a critical path to ensure on-time delivery.* The required sequence of activities and their interdependencies must also be identified and tracked, and preventive action must be taken to avoid failure to meet commitments.

- *Coordinate resources to meet commitments.* The collective actions of in-house cross-functional resources must be orchestrated as well as those of third parties in the value chain to the customer.

- *Ensure quality workmanship.* Each step of the production and fulfillment processes must be managed to attain high-quality delivery (to the customer's specifications) and to remove root causes of any failures to prevent recurrence.

- *Validate with the customer that the commitment has been met.* Customer agreement must be obtained to validate that the commitment was executed to their satisfaction. The performance and outcomes of the associated processes should be measured using metrics of success that customers agree are important and that drive their repeat buying behavior.

2. Enabling infrastructure. The physical things that must be present in the infrastructure to support (enable) the foregoing process capabilities to make and meet commitments include:

- *Organization.* An organizational alignment around the customer, such as by industry for your corporate customers, enables employees to focus on and understand specific customers and their needs, identify how they derive value from your company's products and services, and provide customer-specific product and service delivery.

  Specialization, such as a sales function or customer service center, enables concentration of detailed knowledge for informed judgments regarding products, services, and related commitments.

  Process ownership, via line executives who also have responsibility for critical horizontal processes (e.g., order fulfillment), provides a management focus and ensures that business investments and priorities are made with a cross-functional customer view. The functional specialties mentioned earlier are managed in terms of an overall process flow to the customer.

- *Management and measurement systems.* Formal process management disciplines, such as standardized, documented, and repeatable processes, provide consistent, predictable outcomes and enable employees to make firm commitments. Process measurements and objectives track performance and enable management to identify root causes of missed objectives and take action to prevent recurrence.

- *Customer satisfaction surveys and formalized feedback.* There is no substitute for the voice of the customer. Internal process measurements, although well-intended and often based on extensive business experience and knowledge, do not identify the rapid changes in customer needs or their actual perception of what they received. An airline may "know" it has improved its performance of meeting advertised departure times, but that is irrelevant if customers perceive and believe that flight schedules (commitments) are being missed.

- *Employee objectives and incentives.* When employee objectives and incentives are linked with customer satisfaction and with how well they perform customer-facing processes (designed outside-in to deliver what customers want), the capabilities within these processes to provide value become fully utilized. In this case, valid commitments are consistently made and met.

- *Skills and training.* Formalized training programs and education enable customer-facing personnel to understand the company's products, services, policies, practices, and processes. Mentoring of new hires by experienced peers (as well as prehire peer interviews) also helps ensure the presence of employees with the right prerequisite knowledge and aptitude.

- *Business strategy and practices to target key customer segments.* A strategy to segment customers based on common needs and wants enables the company to organize resources and align knowledge around those customers. Specialized customer-centric organization structure is then possible as well as modular processes that are designed to deliver the specific needs, wants, and customer values of each segment.

- *Information and information technology.* Centralized data regarding companywide products, services, production schedules, and inventory enable customer-contact personnel to identify the right product or service and to commit valid delivery dates. "Deal" databases further allow the capture, retention of, and just-in-time access to those customer commitments and to work in process.

  Formalized employee networking (telephone, e-mail, knowledge sharing) facilitates the communication of commitments and coordination of work in process, cross-functionally. A virtual organization, around a customer set or a company process, may be attained without the need for physical proximity (i.e., without a common department or housing facility).

Applications, such as configuration tools, ensure that only workable combinations of product features are ordered. Workflow-management applications create smart processes that ensure critical process steps are followed, monitor due dates, and track and manage each commitment through to completion. The knowledge resides within the process itself, not only in the heads of highly experienced employees. This enables consistent performance of the processes, even in the presence of high staff turnover and inconsistent employee skills.

The absence of the aforementioned business capabilities and infrastructure can allow invalid commitments to be made or valid ones to be missed and result in severe customer dissatisfaction and attrition. However, when major corporations are assessed against even a skeletal, partial list as in the preceding example, critical gaps are identified and the power of the CVM framework becomes readily apparent.

Customer value management enables a company to:

1. Isolate and focus on the highest leverage customer needs, which drive buying behavior and which require improvement.

2. Determine the specific required business capabilities that they are missing.

3. Focus on the infrastructure elements, which, if provided, would address current missing capabilities, generate customer satisfaction, and increase market share.

Without such a framework, management is left in a sea of internal business objectives and measurement issues, external market dynamics, and a mass of undisciplined customer needs, all of which appear to warrant action, but with no clear path of how or where to proceed. The beauty of CVM is in the eloquence of its simplicity. It is a means to cut through thousands of issues and alternatives to isolate on the critical things that can have a real impact on the business. From the customer's viewpoint, those moments of opportunity for a business to delight them are many.

For example, a moment of opportunity exists every time customers have to give their name, address and account number, and other unchanged boilerplate information more than once during their relationship with a company. Having to do this on a transaction-by-transaction basis sends a message to the customer that the company apparently doesn't know him or her. Yet, a primary reason for customers to want a relationship with a business is often to achieve a comfortable level of familiarity.

Sam: "Beer, Norm?"

Norm: "Am I getting that predictable, Sammy? Good!"

A business that knows its customer is able to ensure that the products and services it provides are matched to that customer's needs. It also can save that customer time with a reduced number of options from which to select (Ms. Smith uses the car only in town, so don't offer her high-speed turnpike tires as an alternative to consider or the roadside service contract). One way to save time is to eliminate unnecessary administrative steps. The television character Norm Peterson always came back to the *Cheers* neighborhood bar because (a) bartender Sam Malone knew he liked beer on tap and (b) he could always get the stool he preferred at the corner of the bar. For a business to demonstrate that type of personalized value, it must have several critical capabilities, such as the ability to recognize an existing customer and the ability to access and use information regarding that customer during a service encounter. Most major businesses are unable to do either one. (Even Sam Malone would actually ask Norm if he wanted a beer!)

When applying for a boat loan at a bank, for example, customers are asked to complete an application that routinely requests information previously provided. It is as if the customer is a complete stranger. In fact, if the customer has a checking account, a home mortgage, and an automobile loan with that bank, the boat loan application will likely request the same data for the fourth time. When you become a patient at a doctor's office, you are asked once for pertinent information. You are not given a clipboard and asked if your father had a heart condition at every subsequent office visit or request for medical service. Well, medical patients are also the customers of corporations. And customers of major corporations, banks for instance, now commonly express their vision that the company ask them for information only once (Figure 7-5).

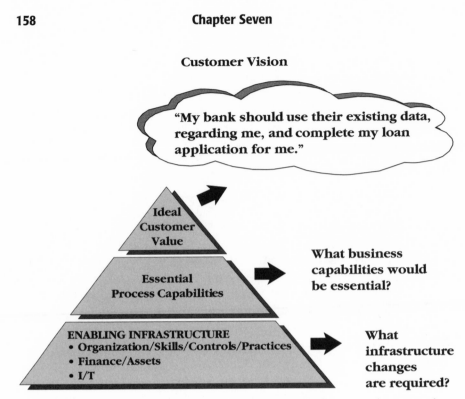

Figure 7-5 Customer vision example: Use my existing information (© Copyright IBM, 1999)

A bank loan department, using a CVM approach to become customer centered, might learn that customers consider using their existing information to be a vision of an ideal financial services provider. To implement this vision, the management team would need to work down the pyramid from that customer-desired outcome to identify the requisite business design.

1. Process capabilities.   For an organization to reuse their existing customer information (in addition to many of the capabilities from the prior examples), they need the following process capabilities:

- *Initial customer-contact personnel capture relationship data once and then make it available bankwide* (Note: unless prohibited by law for banks in your area).

- *Loan-contact personnel understand the data required to approve a loan.*

- *Loan-contact personnel are able to access the customer's information and full relationship with the bank.*

- *Loan-contact personnel are able to transfer customer data to the application.*

2. Enabling infrastructure. This requires some specific things in the bank's infrastructure:

- *Organization.* One-bank alignment around the customer as opposed to the current silo structure organized around bank products allows consolidation of customer data and sharing of data bankwide.

- *Management and measurement systems.* Business process management disciplines, such as standardized procedures to capture and retain customer data during early relationship interactions, enable the downstream processes (e.g., loan application processing) to draw on shared data. Similarly, a standardized, documented loan application process defines the data requirements to be captured by the earlier processes. Process-centric measurements and objectives monitor employee execution of the formal processes.

- *Customer satisfaction surveys and formalized feedback.* Post-transaction surveys monitor customer satisfaction with the loan process as well as with the individual employee's execution of the process.

- *Employee objectives and incentives.* Appraisals, compensation, and rewards linked to loan process-execution metrics and to customer satisfaction provide incentives for customer-centered behavior (i.e., to follow processes and take extra measures to satisfy customers).

- *Skills and training.* Education for both the upstream process bank personnel, such as those involved in opening new customer accounts, and for the loan-contact personnel promotes shared knowledge of how the processes interlock as well as specific knowledge regarding a single process or functional responsibility. The essence of process management is that the output of one function (or process) should be the ideal input of the next one in the value chain. This requires cross-pollination and bankwide awareness of the multisilo, internal bank, customer–supplier relationships.

- *Customer-focused policies and practices.* Loan application contact personnel, empowered to act on behalf of the customer across multiple functional areas, enable the capability to access and transfer appropriate customer data efficiently bankwide.

- *Information and information technology.* A centralized bankwide customer information database, accessible on-line by employees, enables reuse of the information. Smart processes also enable the consistent execution of both the upstream processes (e.g., data capture during earlier interactions) and the loan application process (e.g., access and utilization of existing data) and ensure that all requirements for loan consideration and approval have been met.

So, How Do You Develop the Bottom of the Pyramid?

The pyramid examples (Figures 7-3 through 7-5) illustrate the application of CVM approaches to engineer a tight linkage between what the customer values and what the business can do. The technique to identify these capabilities and infrastructure elements can be best understood as a series of matrices starting with a mapping of customer needs to their respective business capabilities and enabling infrastructure (Figure 7-6). The figure depicts a QFD-like format to capture the linkages and relationships between (a) a menu of customer needs and their required business capabilities and (b) the similar relationships or dependencies between those capabilities and their respective infrastructure enablers. Quality function deployment (QFD) was introduced in Chapter 2 as a framework of matrices that utilize customer requirements to derive product or service design specifications. Customer value management uses similar matrices to link each individual customer need to its required process capabilities and prerequisite infrastructure elements. This identifies a business architecture of capabilities and infrastructure necessary to deliver customer value.

QFD also highlights how a single infrastructure item can enable several different capabilities, which in turn can provide many different

Working Inwards From Customer Needs

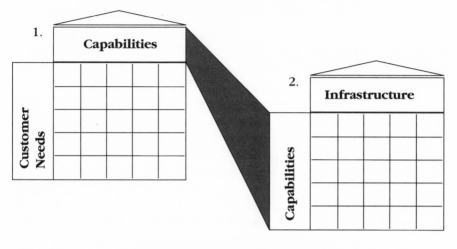

Customer-Centered Enterprise

Figure 7-6 CVM matrices: QFD-like business design (© Copyright IBM, 1999)

CVM Investment Analysis:
Which Infrastructure Items Have the Most Impact?

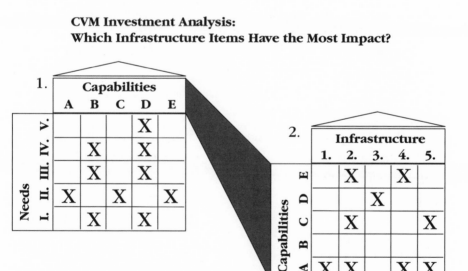

- **Some infrastructure items enable many capabilities**
- **Some of those capabilities deliver many needs**

Figure 7-7 CVM matrices: Analyzing the linkages between infrastructure and needs (© Copyright IBM, 1999)

customer needs. The result in Figure 7-7 is an ability to see that an individual process capability, such as capability D at the top of a column on matrix 1, may relate to and fulfill several customer needs, listed down the side of that matrix. Similarly, in matrix 2 an individual infrastructure element may relate to and enable several different process capabilities.

In the figure, the infrastructure item 3 appears to have the most potential impact on the business, as it links to and enables capability D on matrix 2, which in turn is a requirement for four of five customer needs on matrix 1. In the absence of more information, such as the relative importance of each customer need, infrastructure item 3 warrants consideration as a potential high-value investment item.

In an actual analysis, infrastructure item 3 might be something like a data warehouse of customer information. An example of a capability that this would enable might be the ability to capture and retain a customer history of service calls and preferences. The customer needs, which that capability might help provide, could include "meet your commitments," "provide a service my way," "use my existing information," and so on. A business analysis for each capability (assessing the potential return on investment of the enabling infrastructure, such as a customer database) would include:

- The importance and business impact of the customer needs that depend on this capability.

  Are they the needs with the highest importance and/or greatest performance gaps to be closed with the competition?

  Are they basic needs that must be met or improved to stop attrition?

  Are they attractor needs which a competitor is currently performing at a superior level?

  Would market share increase if the need or needs were provided?

  How much improvement is required?

- The cost of the different alternative means of providing the infrastructure item.

  Cost of manual alternatives (paper logs and recordkeeping).

Cost of automated alternatives (in-house skills and equipment, outsourcing resources).

- The relative return to the business of investing (or impact of not investing) in this item versus the other matrixed infrastructure items.

The data to complete a CVM pyramid and the associated matrices are compiled by utilizing both primary and secondary research techniques and by workshops to facilitate the company personnel who make up the processes (Figure 7-8).

The sources of CVM information include:

- *Business strategy, goals, and objectives.* The company strategy and similar source documents, as well as management interviews, provide excellent starting points for CVM. Information regarding targeted markets and clarification of strategies to compete on either price or value quickly set the framework for the types of data that will be required. These strategic objectives can also be placed at the top of the pyramid in addition to customer-desired outcomes.

Sources of *Customer Value Management* Information

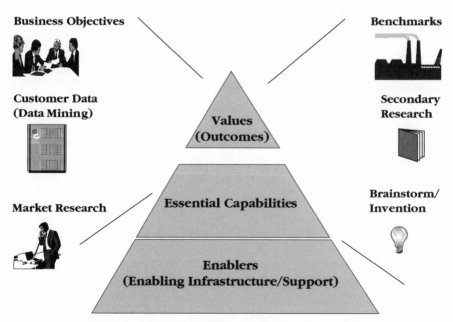

Figure 7-8 Building the pyramid: Sources of CVM data (© Copyright IBM, 1999)

- *Customer transaction data.* Data mining of the firm's own customer transactions provides a rich source of information to identify high- and low-profit target segments, conduct risk assessments, project future profitability, identify common buying behavior, and suggest common value propositions.

- *Primary market research.* Focus groups and quantitative surveys provide a segment-specific customer view to quantify the relative importance levels of each customer need, size performance gaps with competition, and identify behavior drivers for business prioritization.

- *Primary benchmarking.* On-site benchmark visits with companies that customers identify as the best providers of specific needs are a means to identify the underlying capabilities and infrastructure that generate best-of-breed performance. This is particularly beneficial when the benchmarked firm is in a different industry and can point to investments that would establish a new level of performance in the company's industry.

- *Secondary research and benchmarking.* Scanning professional journals (e.g., using the Internet) can provide insights into companies that have distinguished themselves in management literature. By using key words, such as particular needs from the customer-defined vision, other firms can be identified that have demonstrated outstanding capabilities to deliver those needs. Journal articles typically indicate the unique or specific capabilities or enabling infrastructure that account for the company's high performance.

  A CVM study for a major North American corporation scanned 50 published articles about outstanding firms outside of that industry and compiled a robust set of customer service capabilities and infrastructure. These collectively enabled the firm to establish a dramatic new vision and an action plan to attain new industry-leading customer service capabilities. Additional sources of secondary benchmarking are best-practice databases. Organizations such as the American Society for Quality can provide a starter set of performance metrics and best practices for common processes. This initial research can be used to supplement or jump-start cross-functional workshops and brainstorming.

- *Brainstorming.* One of the best sources to identify the middle and bottom portions of the CVM framework is to bring together a team of people who make up the process. For any given customer need that is placed at the top of the pyramid as an outcome of a process or service, there will be a value chain of people who are involved in the delivery of that outcome. Typically, that chain will be cross-functional and comprise at least one enterprise process (e.g., order fulfillment, billing, postsales service, etc.). The people who must fulfill the customer-defined outcome participate in brainstorming workshops to identify the specific capabilities that will be required and the enabling infrastructure that must be present to have those capabilities.

Advanced CVM: Working the Pyramid from the Bottom Up

Once the concepts of CVM and the customer view at the top of the pyramid are clearly understood, they may also be powerfully applied "bottom-up." Customer value management identifies not only what the customer wants but also why. The "why" is the value proposition: how customers derive value or benefit from a process, service, or interaction. This knowledge can be quite powerful when applied bottom up using the framework. For example, if a company finds that the value propositions during interactions with their customers by telephone are speed, convenience, and "saves my time," that information can be used in multiple ways. With conventional, top-down CVM, the insights are used to envision ideal delivery by the current processes. For example, customers are facilitated regarding the ideal telephone service representative or the ideal telephone voice response unit. Then those processes are improved or reengineered to have the capabilities to deliver the customer-envisioned outcomes.

A completely different application would be to have the company personnel identify unique capabilities or infrastructure within the firm that can be used to create new, unexpected delivery of the customer value. That's how today's airline reservations system came about. When American Airlines developed a then-unique automated reservations system not available to customers of other airlines, they were able to take a bottom-up view of the value pyramid and envision the creation of a whole new value proposition using these unique business capabilities. As a result, their SABRE system became the basis, not of a reservations system for the airline, but for a whole new business: the reservations industry. Previously, customers had to call multiple airlines, and they valued each airline's ability to provide accurate information quickly. Thanks to American Airline's unique I/T infrastructure, their employees envisioned a new value pyramid with new high-value outcomes at the top. As a result, American soon made more money from the industrywide use of their reservations capabilities than from flying airplanes.

Applying CVM to Internet Opportunities and Industry Killer Capabilities

The American Airlines transformation was a rare occurrence in that early era of information technology. In today's world, there is rapid emergence of breakthrough technologies, and similar stories are becoming commonplace. The Internet arguably offers the most rapidly developing platform for such killer applications of technology (applications with the potential both to create new industries and to wipe out traditional ones). For every Internet site that tries and fails (and tries again), there is a potential Amazon.com or Yahoo site positioning itself to garner multiple millions of instant customers. Once such sites have the initial customer relationships to lever for scale, they can engineer and expand their capabilities to become e-portals to an unlimited array of new product or service combinations (not just selling books). The firms that combine a CVM pyramid approach with emerging new technological capabilities will create powerful new alignments of infrastructure and customer values. For example, ideal, customer-defined, e-access to a firm's products, services, and information is possible by pursuing such an opportunity both top-down and bottom-up. More important, a whole new array or combination of nontraditional customer-centered products and services is possible.

A top-down pyramid analysis can identify which customer segments are naturally attracted toward doing business via the Internet (within both the consumer and commercial customer sets). For customers who are early adopters of electronic business, the value propositions that attract them can be identified for each electronic moment of truth. Those customers might envision that when they connect to a company electronically, smart processes utilize information they previously provided, eliminating duplicate entry. Better yet, with this electronic customer profile, the ideal vendor can adjust its electronic storefront to display services or merchandise of specific interest to each visitor. For such customers, the company can develop the specific process capabilities and infrastructure required to deliver their top-down vision.

For customer segments that are not inclined toward e-commerce, CVM can be used to identify their must-have needs that are not being provided and that inhibit their use of the Internet. The company could then develop the process capabilities and infrastructure that would correct this and effectively remove barriers to usage as perceived by those segments.

A bottom-up analysis takes the same knowledge of the customer's value proposition at key electronic moments of truth interactions and then considers the new capabilities that could be provided by emerging technology. With the customer's value proposition in mind, the firm envisions how to exploit the new technology or combine it with some unique existing company capability to lever things customers value in a new and creative way. An example is allying with others electronically and using their excess capacity to fulfill customer needs rather than investing in building them.

Recognizing and providing customer preferences are fast becoming commonplace among businesses that know e-commerce. Amazon.com delighted the marketplace with the capability to recommend new titles that appeal to an e-customer's individual area of interest. Tomorrow, such service will become mundane as technology enables dramatic new combinations of capabilities that deliver ever-higher levels of such value.

For example, capabilities now exist for e-commerce via telephone call centers, as outlined in the following section. If applied to an Internet-based transaction, they could be exploited by a creative enterprise to deliver new customer value propositions.

MCI and Others: Using Infrastructure to Create New Capabilities and Values.
High-tech telephone call centers, such as the MCI location I visited on a benchmarking assignment, are generating new value propositions that were envisioned bottom-up by someone who: (a) has insight into the top of the pyramid and what customers will value

and then (b) looks at the possibility to create new capabilities through combinations of new technologies and infrastructure that result in breakthrough delivery of that value.

Some examples of the capabilities available to leading-edge telephone call centers today include:

- Identify where a call originates before the call center answers the telephone.
- Predict who is calling (e.g., a consumer calling from home).
- Search internal databases and compile and analyze the transaction history of the caller such as:

  Language requirements (e.g., someone who speaks only Spanish).
  Purchase history, including patterns and trends.
  Service history and issues.
  Billing and payments history.
  Personal preferences.

- Search externally acquired databases and integrate with internal data for a more extensive profile of the caller's:

  Credit history.
  Risk management assessment.
  Fraud protection assessment.

- Analyze the data and perform predictive modeling, including:

  Current and future value to the company.
  Current call topic and/or future behavior, such as: (a) what the caller is likely to be calling about (past issues; problems the company is having with a product, service, or geography that relates to the customer); (b) whether the caller is likely to want to cancel an existing service; and (c) which products or services the caller is likely to be receptive to purchase (enabling a cross-sell offer while on the phone, although calling on another topic).

- Route the call to a specialist, such as:

  Account savers, who specialize in retaining customers who call to cancel products or services.
  Experts in specific company products or services that may apply.

Language- or geography-specific representatives with special language or cultural skills.

- Present the specialists with both the incoming call and the real-time on-screen data that will enable them to handle the call in a highly personalized manner.

- Network the customer service representative to other databases and to live representatives for real-time access to additional knowledge or information.

- Capture customer issues during the call as input to workflow-management processes that automate and ensure the process steps are completed to manage each customer transaction to completion—in other words, the ability to "meet your commitments."

- Update the customer's individual transaction history so that the next time he or she calls, this information is part of a new analysis for the person receiving the call.

- And more.

Technology can provide companies that do business through electronic commerce (telephone, kiosk, Internet, etc.) with new breakthrough performance capabilities. As more customers go on-line and as their expectations rise regarding e-commerce capabilities, they are providing massive amounts of data about themselves when they enroll for electronic services. This information, coupled with subsequent transaction data, can be used to craft customer value propositions at the time of product or service delivery, as well as feed the management system regarding development and targeting of future new products and services. The data can be provided to tactical front-end sales, customer service, and order fulfillment staff, as well as to the more strategic company functions such as research and development. The customer data can be analyzed with technologies such as data mining and CVM to develop new products and services and for targeted marketing and personalized sales actions, all driven by new infrastructure-enabled capabilities to focus on delivering what customers value.

CVM in Action

The IBM Corporation originally developed CVM to help it become more customer centered and to harness the power of its technology and other infrastructure investments. But the concepts apply to a wide range of business issues, such as in the examples that follow, and do not always require major investments.

Big Bank: Hanging Up on the Customer. When a major retail bank decided to become customer focused and to implement a customer-defined vision, it was concerned that an outside-in approach would only identify things that would cost millions of dollars and take years to implement. A pleasant surprise awaited them. During the very early stages of the work, the CVM practitioners assembled a cross-functional team to demonstrate techniques to brainstorm missing capabilities and infrastructure. The initial customer focus groups had identified an important need that wasn't being met by the bank. Customers wanted to reach a knowledgeable person with only a single transfer when they telephoned. The customers did not expect the first person that answered the phone to have full knowledge of all bank products, services, and processes. But they did expect a bank employee to know who did have this capability, and they did expect to be transferred to that person quickly without multiple subsequent phone transfers. This retail bank had experienced significant growth through mergers (as with our earlier example of a commercial bank). From the customers' perspective, it seemed that bank employees could no longer answer their questions or direct them quickly to someone else who could. Anyone calling this bank faced a formidable task of navigating the constantly changing organizational chart.

A cross-functional group of bank employees met for the first capabilities and infrastructure workshop. Customer value management would be used more extensively later. The workshop was a test. How would the approach work considering the size and complexity of the company? And would the results be practical, actionable, and timely? Or would the workshop generate a white paper containing only expensive recommendations that could never be accomplished in a single lifetime?

The results surprised even the experienced CVM practitioners. As it turned out, when bank employees were asked if they could connect an incoming customer call to a knowledgeable person in single transfer, they all said, emphatically, "No!"

In the course of the workshop, it was revealed that a few critical capabilities (the middle of the CVM pyramid) were not present. For example, bank employees did not know the responsibilities or expertise of many coworkers. In other words, they lacked the capability to identify who in the bank was the right person to handle customer requests or inquiries outside of their own area.

Moving from identifying the capability to facilitating the enabler, the team decided a corporate directory or organization chart was the missing infrastructure item they needed. They felt this could be provided by a simple typed document and updated weekly, or it could be provided by bankwide access to a central employee database cross-referenced by job responsibility. The I/T solution was not a dependency, but it could result in major efficiencies.

When the CVM practitioner asked if such a directory would then enable them to provide the customers' vision of reaching a knowledgeable person in a single transfer consistently, the employees again said, "No."

Although a current organizational directory would enable the capability to identify the correct person, they still lacked the capability to transfer a call to another employee because each individual department had a small telephone budget for incoming calls on their departmental toll-free line. Customers were not charged for these incoming calls, but each department was. If a customer called one department and was subsequently transferred to another, the original department's meter would continue to run. To avoid being charged for another department's calls, their practice was simply to tell the customer to hang up and call the other department. Inane behavior, but true—institutionalized and driven by the bank's measurement system.

The capabilities and enablers workshop determined that the following changes could be made immediately and at low cost. The recommended infrastructure would result in bank capabilities to deliver exactly what their customers wanted:

- A bankwide organization directory.
- A measurement system change to make incoming telephone toll charges no longer a department-level budget objective.
- A business change to establish the practice of a warm transfer (each incoming call is the responsibility of a first point of contact, who stays on the line with the caller during transfers to reach the right knowledgeable person).
- Training on using a directory and on warm transfer procedures.

Finally, at the end of this exercise, the employees were asked, "If you do not know who the correct person is today, then aren't there a lot of misdirected calls?" Their response was that misdirected calls were a major productivity issue. A subsequent analysis revealed that if the bank implemented the recommendations (none of which required major financial commitments), they would avoid $2 to $4 million annually in lost time and productivity. Of course, they would also delight their customers. The bank quickly approved the pilot recommendations and proceeded with the larger study.

The customers of the bank had identified the telephone-banking channel as a major interaction point that could be improved to attract their increased usage and loyalty. In other instances, entire enterprises have been assessed using this type of approach to develop a wider blueprint of the business.

Mexican Distribution Company: NAFTA Is Coming.   When a CEO in Mexico became concerned with the potential impact of the proposed North American Free Trade Agreement (NAFTA), he turned to the CVM approach. NAFTA would result in new entrants into his marketplace. The parent company, a major holding company, controlled several manufacturing firms as well as a distribution company that provided the order fulfillment interface between his factories and his customers. NAFTA would open the borders and let in new competitors, primarily from the north. The CEO feared that these companies, some with world-class capabilities and infrastructure, would provide dramatic new value delivery to the wholesalers and end users of his products (electrical supplies and building materials). This could redefine both the marketplace and call into question his investment to remain in it. He needed to quickly identify the level of investment either to fund a Greenfield project (the construction of a new distribution company with world-class capabilities) or to develop a plan to improve his current processes.

The problem was that he did not know what "world-class" capabilities meant either to his customers (distributors and manufacturers) or to the new competitors. The solution was to utilize CVM and have his customers envision a new distribution company that could ideally meet their needs. The top of the pyramid was provided by the target market segments, primarily distributors and major manufacturers that used his products.

Next came the development of a vision of the middle and bottom portions of the CVM pyramid. The customer-desired outcomes from an ideal distribution firm were used to define the capabilities and infrastructure required. This was accomplished by benchmarking to identify current best practices and by facilitating company personnel to brainstorm creative new ideas.

The result was a model of a new company, an enterprise blueprint, complete with both the customer view and the business view. By estimating the costs associated with the infrastructure (bottom of the pyramid), a rational financial analysis was possible. Building a new company could be compared to the relative costs and timing associated with improving the current one. When the CEO compared his current distribution company capabilities and infrastructure to the ideal model, he determined that the better plan was to use the ideal model as a template for improving the existing company: an end state vision. The current company could be improved and transformed over time by engineering several of the key missing capabilities. Customer value management had given him a rational basis for making his decision.

These anecdotes demonstrate that the best time to use CVM is before any significant infrastructure investment is made. However, a company will often embark on business improvement plans, invest in several initiatives, and then desire to validate its course with a customer view. This is sometimes the case with process reengineering. A process improvement team can generate significant enthusiasm and get down the path of a redesign before having secured an ideal customer view. This type of application of CVM is often iterative. It starts with an internal process improvement team effort to map and analyze the process, and then, in parallel, a team will begin to design the new process almost automatically as part of the analysis and documentation step. It seems that when a team maps a process and identifies the issues, a natural result is a concurrent development of a better process design, even when the work plan calls for the to-be process design as a later step. This often means that a methodical approach to secure the customer view has not yet been done. The urge to do something results in a premature design without the prerequisite customer research. When this occurs, a parallel piece of CVM work should be initiated and then integrated into the process team's design before it becomes final.

British Petroleum: How We Do Things Around Here. British Petroleum (BP), in Australia and New Zealand institutionalized being customer centered. The company developed a cross-functional business process management system and also formalized the approaches into a "how we do things around here" document. The thrust of the document was that being customer-centered and cross-functionally managed was how BP planned to do things.

For example, their order-through-billing, cross-functional activities were analyzed as a horizontal process focused on the ultimate end users. The customers were segmented based on logical groupings, which were likely to have common needs and wants (i.e., distributors, retailers, consumers, etc.). Front-line personnel teams as well as customer panels were established to develop and maintain an ongoing customer view from these segments.

In parallel, the processes were analyzed for nonvalue-add steps as well as opportunities for increased effectiveness. Reengineering teams identified the process capabilities and infrastructure that would be required from an internal perspective for ideal new business processes.

The customer view was then reconciled with and integrated into the design. The reengineering team's initial design and recommendations were validated by the customer vision. In effect, both views were placed at the top of the CVM pyramid. The two views resulted in a powerful business case with both the internal and external customer benefits linked via the capabilities in the middle of the CVM pyramid to the recommended infrastructure investments at the bottom. The infrastructure projects were prioritized and cost justified both by internal cost reductions and by external market impact and projected increased revenues (the desired outcomes). The project was BP's first major exercise that looked at service delivery from a customer, rather than from an internal, perspective. It reportedly turned their thinking around completely and has generated a new customer-centered organization.

The point of these cross-industry examples is that an alignment does not naturally occur or remain between a business's capabilities and the outcomes that its customers value. Markets are dynamic; competitors introduce new offerings; customers experience value in other industries and bring new expectations to you; or as with the bank, you make changes to your own infrastructure (mergers, downsizing, process improvements) and unwittingly lose the balance that may have been present in the past.

Additional issues regarding maintaining balance between business capabilities and customer needs while managing changes are discussed in Chapter 8.

EXERCISE
Applying CVM to Your Business

Management Issues

How has your business drifted away from being tightly aligned with what the customers demand? What new expectations are being set by emerging technologies and new business capabilities in other industries? How could you lever these to create new breakthrough delivery of value for your industry?

1. Capabilities
   - What are the top priority, customer behavior-driver needs that offer greatest bottom-line business return? What new business or process capabilities are required to provide them?
   - What are your customers' issues with your performance? What capabilities and infrastructure will be required to address them?
   - What newly emerging customer expectations are being set by other companies or industries? What are the capabilities of those companies? How could they be adapted to your company or industry?
   - What are your unique capabilities that could be leveraged, working the pyramid bottom-up, to create unexpected value for your customers and a competitive advantage? Or to create a new market?
   - What promises are you making in your branding, advertising, or marketing that are setting expectations that your infrastructure cannot meet?

2. Infrastructure
   - What organization, skills, training, management controls, measurements, incentives, information, technology, business practices, assets, or resources are required to enable the foregoing capabilities?
   - How do these group into rational projects for cost justification and implementation?
   - What new technologies could potentially create breakthrough delivery of the previously mentioned value propositions?
   - How could emerging technologies create totally new capabilities and establish a new value proposition for the industry?

8

Implementation

Balancing Actions, Strategy, and Change Holistically

It is actually not that hard to move from
square processes to new, redesigned round ones.
The hard part is that you still have square people.
HARVEY THOMPSON

Meteorologists are familiar with the theory of chaos. In oversimplified terms, when applied to meteorology, chaos theory refers to the fact that it is impossible to take into consideration all of the variables to make accurate weather forecasts. The seemingly harmless flapping of a butterfly's wings somewhere on the planet could generate a chain of events virtually impossible to predict.

The point is that it is sometimes hard to consider the full "big picture" in your analysis or planning. While reengineering and transforming a major corporation such as IBM is not subject to as many chaotic variables as the weather on planet Earth, still the issues are more far reaching than we realized early in our journey.

When IBM began the trek to become horizontally managed and customer centered, we were certainly unable to see the total big picture. We began by identifying our core enterprise processes at a high level and embarking on a concerted effort to improve their cost and effectiveness. Defect removal, cycle time reduction, and cost improvement were the primary drivers of our early process work, which centered primarily on the activities and workflow within each business process. A more holistic view that incorporated our full business infrastructure, our customers, and our employees became apparent over time as we tried, often failed, and tried again to drive major change into our business. We didn't initially realize the scope and scale of the changes that would be necessary. Simply focusing on how activities flowed across functional organizations and trying to improve these flows to improve our overall business results were tantamount to ignoring the flapping of thousands of butterfly wings.

For example, functional units tightly manage most traditional business enterprises. At that time, there was little capture or analysis of the cross-functional costs that collectively represent a major cross-functional business process. Management systems are typically not aligned horizontally, and accounting systems almost always are not. And like all big businesses, IBM had a myriad of products and service offerings that were often supported or delivered by complex, common processes such as sales, manufacturing, distribution, billing, and postsales service. The large, common processes were both a strength (leveraging efficiencies of scale and mass production) and a weakness (obscuring the costs associated with the support of individual products, services, internal organizations, or customers).

For example, to consider how to take cost out of the process support of a product, it was necessary to know how much it cost to handle very different products with the common core processes. How much less did it cost to process a customer order for a PC than for a mainframe? Or did it cost the same if the same order process was used? And if it did cost the same, could we afford to use our mainstream order processes for lower margin products or services? And what about adding feature options to new products or services, which in turn add complexity to the support processes? How many more steps would an additional product feature or contract option add to the total process costs to order, build, distribute, invoice, or maintain it? If these costs were known, would certain low-margin products or features suddenly require unique lower cost processes? Or would the price need to be increased? And so on. And this was before we even began to consider the potential impacts or dependencies that new or changed processes would have on our company culture, our employees, and our customers. All potential butterfly wings.

Looking at the situation with hindsight, it is apparent that the theory of chaos was playing havoc with IBM's efforts. Major corporations typically face such issues as symptoms of their size. IBM believed that horizontal business process management was the vehicle to resolve those issues and to gain cross-functional efficiencies. We have since learned that such an analysis and redesign of a horizontal process are only one piece of a larger holistic set of relationships, which includes the various elements of the business, the marketplace, and our employees.

Fortunately, business process improvement, although more difficult than we initially imagined, is not totally subject to the theory of chaos. Many of the key variables affecting a business enterprise can be identified, categorized, placed into a hierarchy, and managed. However, the key is to understand the most critical of those elements and to establish and then manage changes to them holistically (Figure 8-1).

For a company to become and to remain customer centered require a balanced holistic approach. IBM's first step was to identify its own core processes and perform an initial mapping and assessment of their current state. Initial activities were focused to make each process more efficient by removing nonvalue-add steps and

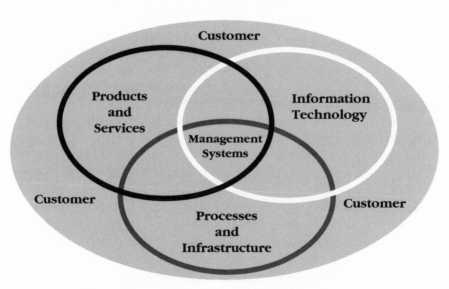

Challenge: Maintain Alignment With the Customer

Figure 8-1 Holistic change: Keeping the pieces in balance (© Copyright IBM, 1999)

adding audits and edits to ensure that what came out of the process was as intended. The employee buy-in to perform these redesigned processes didn't occur until it became apparent that the future viability of IBM (and of the employees' jobs) hinged on the implementation of sustained changes that meet the needs of customers. Customer value management approaches were then developed to engineer a business that aligned with those needs of the customer. Creative and innovative customer-focused methods resulted in the development of new customer-facing processes, such as customer relationship management, customer order fulfillment, and billing. However, these processes were only one component of the overall business system.

The challenge is to calibrate and align all the major elements of the business, as depicted in Figure 8-1, so they are mutually supportive, holistically balanced, and aligned and linked with the things that drive customer buying behavior. Once an alignment and balance are attained, however, the reality is that the environment will not remain constant. Some butterfly is going to flap its wings. More specifically, changes will take place that must be integrated or absorbed into the business without upsetting that balance. For example, when cost reduction pressures occur, how do you manage change into the processes to reduce their cost by, say, 25 percent without losing their alignment with the customers' vision of an ideal vendor? Or how do you replace outdated infrastructure or introduce new technologies while maintaining the service levels required by target market segments? How do you implement those major changes without losing control or without losing employee buy-in and motivation? What about responding to changes in the marketplace, such as the introduction of new competitive offerings? Or to changes in customer needs or their perceptions of your performance versus that of the competition?

Many of these change issues could sustain a book in themselves. For now, I will identify only some of the key points regarding a holistic approach to become customer focused rather than a complete tutorial on organizational change.

To begin, major change requires a vision of a desired to-be end state, which is clearly defined and easily communicated and understood. To be successful, a business vision must include a logical set of elements that are aligned, linked, and managed holistically to accomplish the desired outcomes (Figure 8-2). Customer value management provides an excellent foundation for such a vision, grounded in very specific customer-defined attributes.

Figure 8-2 reflects much of what we have learned to become a successful customer-centric company. It begins with an understanding of your current piece-parts. The puzzle, however, fails to adequately capture the complexity and number of components of a business. In most large business enterprises, there are literally thousands of elements: business visions, missions, strategies, products, services, measurements, objectives, competencies, functions, organizations and departments, processes, procedures, policies, practices, controls, skills, training, incentives, culture, physical assets, financial assets, intellectual assets, and on and on. Once, long ago, all of those various components may have fit together nicely. Possibly that was when the organization was young and the customers made

The Journey Toward Alignment

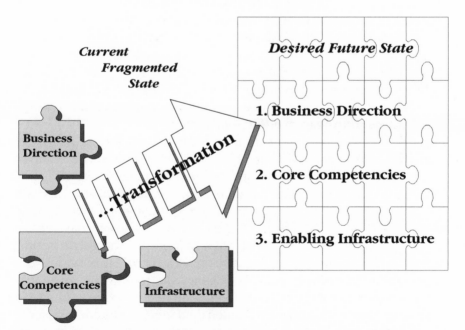

Figure 8-2 Holistic change: Making the pieces fit together (© Copyright IBM, 1999)

fewer demands and everyone in the company knew what everyone else was doing. But times change. The world becomes more complex. Competitors introduce new offerings. Parallel, noncompeting industries introduce new value perceptions to customers. And the customers' needs change. In an attempt to keep up, the business makes changes in an ad hoc, undisciplined manner.

As the customers' expectations change in terms of the outcomes of a business, the business's products, services, and processes also change, often only just in time and at the very end of a series of processes at the point of interaction with the customer. When the output of a customer-facing process is modified to meet new customer demands, often the prior upstream process steps or activities (or upstream supplier processes) no longer tightly align with the requirements of that downstream, modified customer-facing process. For example, if distribution is changed to accommodate customers' expectations for personalized shipment and delivery, then distribution may need radically different information from other upstream processes such as manufacturing. Manufacturing in this case may also have new dependencies on the sales process to secure and provide the new or additional customer-preference data.

If businesses continuously monitored dynamic market requirements and managed (reengineered) internal changes to ensure they were in alignment with the new needs, then each process in the value chain would continuously be modified to provide ideal input to the others. However, this type of a holistic approach is almost universally absent. Instead, we find that each process within a business tends to add staff to reconcile and uplift the no longer adequate input received from the other processes. Over time, those component puzzle pieces, or elements that make up the business, drift apart and no longer fit tightly together. The output of process A does not keep up with the changes and new requirements for ideal input to process B. And collectively, the gaps (white spaces) that appear between the processes are bridged with nonvalue-add headcount, which adds cost and drains the efficiency of the organization.

The point of CVM is to provide a framework to transform that current-state picture of a fragmented, misaligned puzzle of business piece-parts into a holistically aligned and tightly linked customer-centric enterprise. Figures 8-2 and 8-3 contain two such messages. One is horizontal on the graphic and depicts the journey that must take place from a disjointed, irrational business model to an aligned and linked model. The other message is vertical on the graphic, as the desired end state is depicted as a CVM-like alignment among business direction, business competencies or capabilities, and infrastructure.

Business Direction

Well-articulated business direction and a clear statement of where we are going are required to help employees understand and agree on common goals. It is not possible to write an employee manual for every potential business situation. In lieu of such a rule book, a company that truly wants to become customer centered must provide its employees with statements of business direction that provide a framework for decision making. If the employees understand the

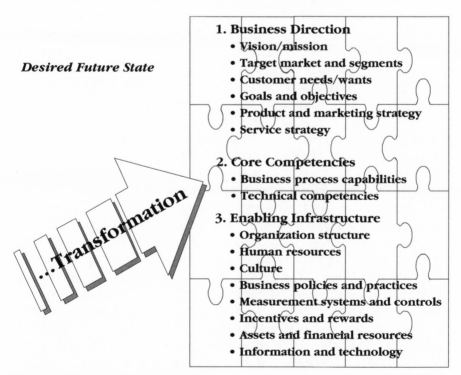

Figure 8-3 Desired future state: Alignment and linkages (© Copyright IBM, 1999)

business vision and mission statements, they have a context of what is important to the company to guide their behavior. Further, by identifying the supporting core competency and infrastructure depicted in Figure 8-3, not only are employees guided in their behavior (e.g., the Disney World example in Chapter 7), but the actual engineering of the business capabilities and infrastructure becomes possible. A vision of tightly linked and aligned piece-parts can be attained, assuring the capabilities to accomplish the business direction at the top.

A to-be end state vision is anchored by a well-articulated set of values, vision, and mission for the organization. While this may sound trite, the fact is that many major organizations attempt to manage significant change by starting at the bottom of the puzzle in Figure 8-3. Often, company executives will ask management consultants or I/T consultants to embark on huge infrastructure transformation projects without regard to the fundamentals expressed in the figure. The more clearly the top of the puzzle is defined in terms of business direction, the better the possibilities to construct the necessary capabilities and infrastructure. In addition, the more precise the desired outcomes are defined at the top of the model, the higher the probability of a return on investment from the infrastructure subsequently designed at the bottom.

Business direction includes both the internal view of vision, mission, goals, and strategy as well as an external view. Here is where companies almost always fall short, even those with well-articulated business direction. They fail to define clearly for whom they are in business. Customer value management calls out the need to clarify desired targeted customers and then to use these customers' views as a major element of the business direction by reconciling the company and the customer views for a holistic business vision. If an enterprise has a mission or vision statement to be "the preferred provider of X to our customers," the next questions are: For whom? What are your targeted market segments? What is their vision of an ideal you? What business strategies, goals, objectives, metrics of success, products, and services are required to attract and retain them? This information serves to add clarity, depth, and focus to the internally defined business direction and enables the subsequent customer-centric definition of the next two vertical portions of the puzzle in Figure 8-3: capabilities and infrastructure.

Core Competencies and Capabilities

Once the top of the puzzle has been well defined, then the middle section, which correlates to the middle of the CVM pyramid, can be defined. We are integrating the customer view with the business view. Remember that many such capabilities may already exist, but in a disjointed current state. These may no longer apply to the customers' current needs, or they may be somewhat out of alignment with other more recent capabilities that depend on them. Again, to manage change, a holistic view must be maintained. In this case, the term *critical success factors* may be substituted, if you like, for process capabilities—the critical few things that must go well to achieve the business direction. Those factors might include technical competencies, such as low-cost, small-engine manufacture or high-volume audio/video miniaturization, and a robust set of business process capabilities, such as the ability to provide electronic access to customers or ensure overnight delivery.

Infrastructure

It is the infrastructure that provides the capabilities, which in turn deliver the desired outcomes to accomplish the business direction (Figure 8-3). Unfortunately, an infrastructure is insidious. It is relatively easier to create one than it is to take one away once it is no longer needed. For example, over the past few years, how many new measurements or procedures have you seen introduced in your own place of business? Probably several. Now, how many others have you seen eliminated because they are no longer relevant? Probably none. Virtually everything that has ever been introduced into the processes, policies, procedures, practices, and controls of a department remains today. For example, consider the fact that many local and state laws stay on the books long after they are needed, such as the one in Connecticut that requires the highest elected official to, once a year, walk around the border of the town or city where they preside. It probably made sense in some prior environment.

I once heard Dr. Michael Hammer tell how his wife always cut the ends off a roast before placing it into the oven. He said he watched this ritual for years and finally one evening was moved to ask why. His wife replied, "Because my mother always cut the ends off the roast." Unsatisfied, Dr. Hammer suggested they call his mother-in-law to find out why she did this. The mother-in-law explained that in her early married days her kitchen was small and she had only a single little oven. She had cut off the ends of the roast in order to get it to fit into the small cooking pans that she had acquired as a newlywed. Somehow, that practice had continued up through the years, to the point that it had become institutionalized within the family, with no one remembering why it was done or questioning that it no longer applied to the current environment.

In another example, the current-state flow of a paper process in an insurance company included routing international policies though a particular desk that had no visible added value. When the topic was pursued, it was learned that, early in the company's history when it started doing business internationally, the only person who spoke a foreign language sat at that particular desk. Over the years, as the company's international business blossomed, the original reason for that workflow was forgotten, but the process of routing paper to that desk had become institutionalized, regardless of the fact that the woman who initially did the translations had long since retired. As the business changed, the laborious practice was continuously modified to include new business offerings, although the original reason for the process step no longer existed.

That is the insidious nature of infrastructure! It is hard to get rid of a procedure once it is institutionalized. As a result, even though the old process hardly makes sense today, everyone in the business continues making quick-fix modifications so that the process works, albeit ham-handed, in the new environment. Typically, this effort includes the addition of nonvalue-add staff to bridge the current gaps. This occurs for both the small activities as well as the larger multiactivity processes. And over time, the piece-parts of the business (still there, even though they have ceased making sense) no longer fit together efficiently or effectively. Figure 8-3 depicts the potential benefits that can be attained by using CVM to define a to-be state where the pieces fit tightly together.

IBM: Taking 200,000 People Out of the White Space. When CVM and holistic change are employed, great things are possible. A business that moves from a current state with disjointed piece-parts to a holistic vision of tightly aligned and linked business components effectively eliminates the white spaces that develop over time between the different parts. For example, when the sales process is redesigned so that its outputs are the ideal inputs for an efficient and effective downstream order process, savings are gained. The people who formerly occupied the white spaces between the two processes are no longer required. Nonvalue-add activities are eliminated because there is no longer a need to correct and uplift the quality of output of one process so that it might be used by another. As a result, fewer staff are required, at a lower cost, to attain a higher level of customer value and satisfaction. People often ask how IBM was able to remove approximately 200,000 people from its payroll, while at the same time accomplishing huge financial and business benefits (customer satisfaction went up over 4 percent and shareholder value went up tenfold). I say it was simple—we took them out of the white spaces—but I do not say it was easy. And the journey is not over!

So if it ultimately worked at IBM, why have others tried and failed? For starters, all of our efforts did not initially result in great success. We had to learn over time what did and did not work. In light of what we have learned, it is now possible to go back and look at the hotel chain and the power and light company that were cited in Chapter 2.

The hotel chain example from Chapter 2 can be better understood by looking at Figure 8-4. What happened? The hotel understood very well what was of value to their customers. The hotel had focused on the customer and aligned their products and services by announcing a new value proposition of a guaranteed no surprises, defect-free stay. Unfortunately, it couldn't deliver on that promise. Television sets didn't work, lights were burned out, and other surprises awaited guests. This value proposition was unattainable because, at the time, the hotel lacked holistic change management. Therefore, their process capabilities, such as identifying and committing an inventory of available rooms, and their enabling infrastructure, such as a global reservations system, weren't aligned and tightly linked to their promise to provide what customers wanted. Today, that company has made great advances by also addressing their infrastructure.

The power company example from Chapter 2 can be understood by looking at Figure 8-5. The utility attempted to take a holistic view of the company. They effectively managed the different internal elements

So, what went wrong at the hotel chain?

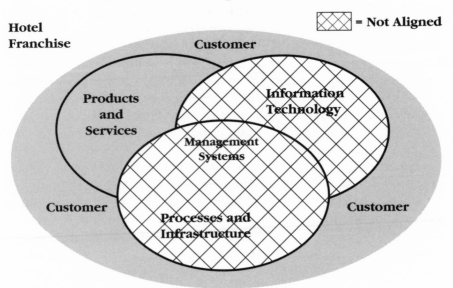

Figure 8-4 Simple to say, hard to do: What about the hotel chain? (© Copyright IBM, 1999)

And, what happened with the power company?

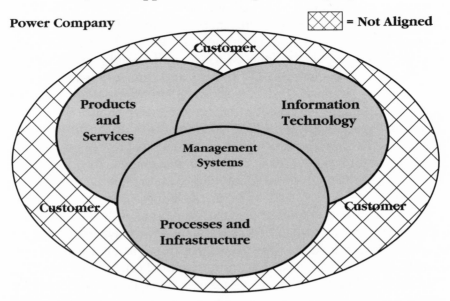

Figure 8-5 Simple to say, hard to do: What about the utility company? (© Copyright IBM, 1999)

of their business with a balanced approach for total quality management (TQM). But missing was inclusion of the customer into that view. The piece-parts of the business were balanced and worked well together to jointly attain the stated business direction, which included company-defined customer metrics. Unfortunately, no one asked the customer if these measurements were important. The result was that the metrics were attained but were not aligned with what the customers valued.

The point is that holistic change management requires a firm to take the full view of all the interrelated elements of the business and its component parts. As these examples demonstrate, a holistic, balanced view includes both the company and the customer. These two views must be successfully integrated, and when they are in conflict, they must be reconciled.

Figure 8-6 demonstrates a reconciliation of a company's business direction with the needs, wants, and values of a targeted customer. In the figure a company has a stated business direction that includes being the low-cost provider and also dealing with the customer through a single channel. The customers, on the other hand, have expressed needs including a desire for value-add support services (not compatible with the company vision of low-cost commodity provider) and for a direct access channel (not compatible with the company vision of a single dealer channel). In this situation, which actually occurred with a major North American firm, the company faced a choice either to sacrifice this specific market segment overtly or to modify the company direction to become compatible with the needs of that group of customers. The CEO wisely elected to modify the business strategy to be compatible with the desires of this potential high-growth customer segment.

Square to Round People

Designing the new round (customer-driven) processes to replace old square ones does not end the journey; the challenge is how to maintain an alignment with customers while changing the processes, the support infrastructure, and the behavior of the people who implement the processes. Note: The infrastructure element must include the company's people. This alignment is where the vision becomes reality.

When the Company and Customers Disagree

Strategic Alignment

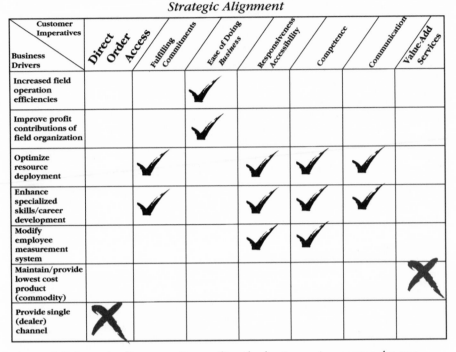

Business Drivers \ Customer Imperatives	Direct Order Access	Fulfilling Commitments	Ease of Doing Business	Responsiveness Accessibility	Competence	Communication	Value-Add Services
Increased field operation efficiencies			✓				
Improve profit contributions of field organization			✓				
Optimize resource deployment		✓		✓	✓	✓	
Enhance specialized skills/career development		✓		✓	✓	✓	
Modify employee measurement system				✓	✓		
Maintain/provide lowest cost product (commodity)							✗
Provide single (dealer) channel	✗						

Figure 8-6 Strategic alignment: Reconciling the business view versus the customer view (© Copyright IBM, 1999)

Once the holistic picture has been defined, the customer needs have been reconciled with the business direction, and the business processes have been designed to align and link with customers' needs, the employees of the company must take ownership of the new processes. In many cases, the new ways of doing things will require significant changes in the behavior of the employees who collectively perform the processes. The fact that the processes were designed based on the voice of the customer is often a positive motivator that can sustain a new process and secure employee buy-in. Negative motivators, of course, are another means to secure employee buy-in, such as, "We will be out of business unless we change." If the business is in crisis and is losing customers, then negative motivators will often overcome resistance and drive a willingness to change.

A better way to secure a sustained change in behavior, however, is to engage the employees in the actual redesign effort and then to align employee compensation, incentives, and rewards with the performance of the new process. Process measurements and metrics can be linked to individual employees or to team performance. The most powerful approach in terms of sustained behavior, employee buy-in, and business impact is to further link employee compensation and rewards to customer satisfaction measures. The customer satisfaction metrics, in turn, must be tied to customer opinion or satisfaction surveys that measure the things, which—if performed particularly well—will drive improved customer loyalty and market share. Thus, CVM is executed holistically to engineer customer-centric business processes and to institutionalize them by creating a customer-focused employee culture.

Reaping the Benefits of Being Customer Centered at IBM. In the case of IBM, during our initial efforts to transform the company, a senior executive said, "We have a one-third, one-third, one-third situation here. Approximately one-third of our employees just don't get it. Another third get it but don't know what to do. And a final third get it but just don't want to do it. We can work with the first two groups, but by the time this is fully implemented, the third group will no longer be with the company." Major actions were then undertaken to help the employees get it. These included:

- Orchestration of communications and educational programs to ensure our people clearly understood the changes that were required for our company and the employees' role in making those changes happen.

- Elevating the customer to the position of final arbiter, whose judgment determined whether our performance was satisfactory or not.

- Implementation of new programs that rated and ranked employees based on both their individual and team contributions toward attaining customer-focused goals and objectives. Executives, whose compensation had previously been 80/20 skewed toward business unit operational objectives versus overall company results and customer satisfaction, found that ratio reversed in the new environment. Customer satisfaction and employee compensation moved closer together than ever before.

Ultimately, the culture changed and aligned around a new set of values and vision for the company. The results have been extraordinary, and while they will no doubt be dramatically different (and ideally, even better) by the time this manuscript is published, some of the results achieved between 1994 and early 1999 by round people in new round processes include:

- Changed the IBM company and employees from a product focus to a customer focus.

- Changed from function-driven to process-driven operations.

- Defined and reengineered core business processes including:

  Market management
  Customer relationship management
  Integrated product development
  Procurement
  Integrated supply chain
  Production
  Order fulfillment
  Human resources
  Information technology
  Finance

- Improved business performance, specifically:

  Customer satisfaction up 5.5 percent
  Product development cycle reduced 75 percent
  Win rate up significantly (proprietary data)
  Revenue increased from $63 billion to over $80 billion
  Employees reduced from 409,000 to 220,000
  Monthly financial close reduced from 26 days to 6 days
  Cost and expense savings $= -\$7$ billion to date
  Stock price improved over 1000 percent

Clearly, by following customer-centric, horizontal process management disciplines such as CVM, IBM and the many companies cited as examples in Chapters 1 through 8 have attained quantum leaps in business performance.

The concepts covered up to this point in the book have to do with how to understand who your customers are, what they want and value, and how to align your business with them. If the dynamics stopped at that point and nothing ever changed, you would be in perfect alignment with your customers. However, a major premise of CVM is that things do change—who your customers are, what their value is to you, what they need and want, and what your business capabilities must be—and additional disciplines are required to monitor and adapt to these changes.

How to institutionalize being customer centered (and ensure you do not drift apart from your customer or lose the hard-won benefits gained in Chapters 1 through 8) is discussed in Chapter 9.

EXERCISE
Applying CVM to Your Business

Management Issues

How do you identify and manage the critical success factors to become a customer-centered company? How do you sustain the changes that will be required?

1. Holistic view
   - Do you have a clearly defined and communicated end state vision for the organization?
   - Is it both company- and customer-defined?
   - Who are the outside customer segments that must be considered?
   - What are the elements within your business where change must be managed (people, products, services, processes, infrastructure) in order to attain the vision?
   - How often do you "revisit" these questions to ensure your CVM efforts are on track?

2. Alignment and linkages
   - Does your stated business direction include a company vision, mission, target markets, products and offerings, and (customer-defined) metrics of success as design points?
   - What is the customer view of their needs and wants, behavior drivers, and improvement priorities for your organization? Of your organization versus the competition?
   - What is the strategic alignment of the company view versus the customer view? Do company goals, objectives, critical success factors, products, offerings, processes, and metrics of success align and agree with customer needs and behavior drivers?
   - Do employee objectives, measurements, and incentives align and link with the foregoing? Are hiring practices, jobs, skills, education, and training aligned?
   - Does the vision include both a measurable set of business objectives and the CSFs (i.e., capabilities and infrastructure changes) necessary to attain them?

- What are the gaps or white spaces between the piece-parts of your business? What savings can be accomplished by eliminating the gaps and the nonvalue-add work to bridge them? Where are you cutting the ends off the roast? What if you stopped?

3. Change management
   - Are the foregoing communicated, understood, and agreed to by the employees?
   - Is the need for sustained change understood? Is change grounded in a clear company- and customer-defined vision? Are measures and incentives aligned with change objectives?

9

Maintenance

Sustaining CVM, Always

*Every 24 hours the world turns over on
whoever was sitting on top of it yesterday.*
BASEBALL MANAGER GEORGE "SPARKY" ANDERSON

You're ready. You have followed the approaches outlined in Chapters 1 through 8, and you have arrived at a customer-defined end state for your business. Your marketplace has been segmented into groups of customers based on their current and future value and then subsegmented into clusters of customers with common needs and wants. Target market segment needs have, in turn, been divided into buying behavior drivers and prioritized based on their relative potential to improve your business. Your business capabilities and enabling infrastructure have been redesigned to align and link with the customers' vision of ideal delivery of those needs where financially appropriate. Your employees participated in the redesign. They understand the need for change, and their individual metrics of success and compensation are now based on new behavior and on overall customer satisfaction. Yesterday was the opening day for the new customer-defined processes, and your customers loved them. Congratulations!

Now, get set to do it again. Today, you are one day out of sync with your customers. In the past 24 hours, the world has changed and so have your customers' needs, wants, and perceptions of you and of your competition. The competition is announcing new offerings. Your customers have had their expectations reset by an advertisement from a competitor or perhaps by a service experience with a completely different industry. Or possibly their customers have experienced one of these, and now your customers' customers are making new demands on them. And the exciting new business capabilities and infrastructure of yesterday no longer fit your customers' needs today. The puzzle pieces that make up your business, and which must align and link with your customers, have already begun to drift apart.

How do you handle this and manage to stay in sync? Should you add staff to prevent the white spaces from appearing between the pieces? Should you wait a year or two and do another CVM analysis and reengineer? Or perhaps put your head in the sand like an ostrich and hope the tiger will go away?

Up until this point in the book, our customer-value-based approach has been presented as a method to attain alignment between your business and what the customers want. While that is true, CVM is not a one-time event. It is an ongoing process to maintain a customer-centered enterprise. Once a customer-defined vision has been attained by a business or by an individual process, that vision must be continuously monitored and updated as customers' needs and perceptions change. Formal, repeatable, and continuous processes for CVM are required to proactively sense changes in the marketplace and effectively respond by managing the corresponding changes into your business capabilities (Figure 9-1). The figure depicts several ongoing CVM subprocesses which comprise an overall set of capabilities to monitor the marketplace, identify changes in customer needs, and manage the corresponding change into the business:

- *A customer-requirements subprocess* is a set of formal, documented procedures that regularly analyze the needs of targeted market segments. These include, but are not limited to:

  Segmentation analyses and retargeting. A customer and transaction database provides the capability to mine millions of business interactions and, coupled with analyses of purchased outside databases, to reassess your segmentation and targeting. Risk assessments, current and future customer value projections, buying behavior, and other analyses can be conducted, and the target segments revalidated or changed.

Customer Value Management Process

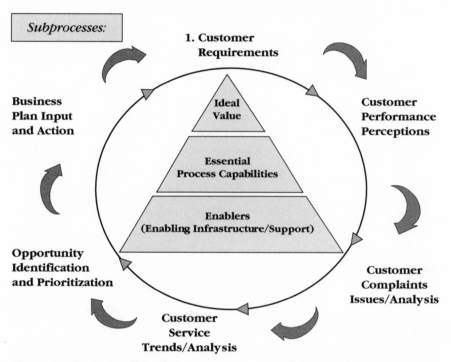

Figure 9-1 Institutionalizing being customer centered: The CVM process (© Copyright IBM, 1999)

Needs and wants monitored by segment. Customer councils, front-line customer-facing employee teams, and qualitative customer focus groups provide formal vehicles to monitor and update the business vision with the voice of the customer.

Behavior-driver categorization of needs. The customer-needs categories of basic must-haves, satisfier nice-to-haves, and attractors that differentiate the business are fluid and must be monitored to identify when items move from one category to another. The differentiators of today will become the basic needs of tomorrow. In the 1970s, am/fm stereos with tape cassettes were attractors in new cars. Today, they are a basic expectation; CD players and enhanced sound systems are the high-value audio features. In the 1980s, automatic teller machines (ATMs) with a global network and worldwide access were differentiators for some banks. Today, global ATM networks are a basic expectation of mobile customer segments, such as business travelers, and a must-have requirement for all banks. The more powerful and desirable a high-value differentiator/attractor is, the more likely it will become a basic expectation over time. Competitors must provide it or concede market share. As a result, it evolves to become widely available and a common offering, which the customers learn to expect from all vendors. The business that does not monitor changing customer value perceptions, and know when that transition occurs, can suffer greatly as an item moves from an optional business offering to a requirement to remain in business.

Strategic vision of customer-defined ideal value delivery. As new customer segments are tagged as being of high future value to the company, their visions of ideal value delivery from the company must be identified and incorporated into the business investment plan. Existing high-value customers must also be monitored for changes in their expectations and in their dynamic vision of what will be ideal over the strategic period. This requires formal, methodical processes to obtain input from customers and prospects (e.g., "customer visioning sessions") to project their needs over the upcoming strategic period, identify business improvement opportunities, and update the business plan.

- *A customer-performance perceptions subprocess* is a set of formal activities and documented procedures to obtain quantitative performance metrics from customers. This area includes:

Ongoing customer satisfaction surveys. A statistically representative sampling of each target market segment must be polled regularly. The dynamics and rate of change of the industry should determine the timing of surveys. A manufacturer of locomotive engines, for example, will have a more stable marketplace than a provider of financial services and may require less frequent customer surveys. Companies in industries where customer expectations are dynamically reset by services on the Internet, such as stock and mutual fund brokerages, must maintain a very current outlook on their marketplace. Questions on surveys by these industries must be regularly modified to reflect current customer needs, wants, and expectations. Subprocesses to do this will typically generate targeted surveys both to customers and to prospects (to secure performance perceptions of competitors by their customers). These may be by mail, telephone interview, in person (e.g., shopping mall interviews), or on-line. Such surveys enable an ongoing gap analysis that reflects the company's performance of customer-behavior-driver needs versus the performance of key competitors.

Event-driven customer surveys (e.g., posttransaction, immediate callback by an interviewer) after a product or service interaction. Satisfaction surveys are typically conducted by a third party. However, customer-centered companies sometimes have trained staff specialists who monitor live telephone sales and service calls or who conduct personal follow-up calls to determine customer satisfaction. The monitoring of employees' conversations with customers during service calls is a routine practice in the United States, particularly for telephone sales or financial services transactions, but this can be prohibited in some countries. Actual customer feedback is usually preferred over the impressions of an internal employee monitor. While there is no substitute for the actual customer's feedback, some companies effectively combine both an internal person to monitor and assess a sampling of telephone service calls and an additional smaller follow-on telephone survey of some of those same customers. By correlating the surveyed customers' satisfaction responses with the internal monitor's assessment of those same service calls, the techniques used by the monitor to assess calls can be compared, calibrated, and aligned with the values used by customers. This results in a reliable low-cost technique to monitor subsequent calls internally that is credible and validated by external customers.

Mailings may also be conducted after a product or service delivery event as well as surveys enclosed with the products, often in the form of a postcard attached to the product or service registration or warranty information. Web response forms allow Internet customers to easily provide feedback on-line immediately following a transaction.

- *A customer-complaint subprocess's* primary objective is rapid response and issue handling. However, a company that practices CVM will also include trend analysis, root cause determination, and corrective action to prevent a recurrence of the issue. Customer-centered companies ensure a closed-loop feedback system is in place to inform the customer that corrective action has been taken.

  Customer complaints should also be analyzed and exploited as a major source to identify newly emerging market needs or changes in current customers' perceptions of company performance of high-leverage needs. In this case, the customer or market has come to you with valuable research information. One of the criteria to identify which customer needs are the basic must-haves is that customers often complain when these needs are not met (e.g., phone calls not returned, rental cars not available, television not working in a hotel room, etc.). Essentially, a complaint-handling process is a channel for customer-initiated market research.

- *A customer service subprocess* should also have multiple roles. One obvious purpose of customer service is the responsive delivery of whatever the customer has contacted the company to obtain, such as action regarding their account or information on products and services. Another role is to analyze these requests as precursors and indicators of emerging customer needs and wants.

  A major manufacturing and distribution company in Asia, for example, was focused on handling customer service calls by treating them as expense items and defects. Their intent was to get head count and costs to remain flat for the customer service call center as their call volumes grew. Process reengineering and automation were merely viewed as enablers to reduce customer service expense. When CVM was implemented, however, the perception of customer service changed from being merely a cost center and overhead to an investment. By also designing the customer service call center capabilities to meet their customers' basic and attractor needs, the manufacturer turned the project into an investment to improve customer satisfaction and loyalty.

Good customer service not only drives increased customer satisfaction and loyalty via customer value delivery, but it is also an excellent source of market intelligence. The customer call center in Asia was reengineered to become a data collection point for information regarding the individual customer. Service call data were retained in the customer information database for analysis to segment prospects for targeted marketing programs and to identify emerging trends in customer needs and wants. The firm learned to use its existing customer data gathered during incoming customer service calls to monitor changes in the marketplace rather than rely solely on formal, costly third-party research. The reengineering became much more than a cost-cutting project. By capturing and analyzing the transaction data from these interactions, the firm was also able to identify emerging customer-performance issues or changing market needs for input to product development.

- *An opportunity identification and prioritization subprocess* converts the top of the CVM business model or pyramid (customer-desired needs and values) into a set of business priorities for focused investment decisions regarding the middle (business capabilities) and bottom of the pyramid (enabling infrastructure). This can be a manual subprocess regularly performed by the firm's CVM experts to pinpoint improvement actions. For example, Chase Bank has a CVM group function headed by a senior vice president of CVM to ensure the correct organizational skills and focus are in place for the enterprise. This can also be a highly automated process (as enabled by tools such as IBM's Dynamic CVM application). No matter how it is performed, a methodical, systematic approach should be institutionalized to capture and analyze the data from these subprocesses, identify performance improvement requirements from the outside-in, and convert these into business design criteria to address missing capabilities and infrastructure. These must be formulated into cost-justified projects, such as new technologies, changed organizational structures, and revised processes.

■ *A business financial plan subprocess* must be initiated or modified to include two major, customer-centered elements:

Business process owners should have the authority and responsibility to improve the business via cross-functional actions and investments based on a holistic, enterprisewide view. In other words, the interests of each individual vertical function, or silo, within the business must be subsumed to meet the greater interests of the enterprise and the needs of the external customer. This must be done with an executive management focus on the horizontal flow of activities, cross-functionally and cross-silo, to the external customer (via enterprisewide business processes).

Often, when companies embark on process management as a means of controlling internal costs or to deliver customer needs and wants, the first step is to identify core business processes and then assign these to senior staff, not to line management, for ownership. When line management and enterprise process staff management conflict, and they will, the power in that scenario resides with line management and effectively negates the advantages of process management as a vehicle for holistic, enterprisewide improvement. There are many alternative models and management systems to deal with this conflict. Our experiences, having implemented process management in industries such as information processing, petroleum, financial services, telecommunications, and automotive manufacturing, have shown that there is no single formula for success. In IBM's journey, a major success factor was when the responsibility for process improvement was assigned to vertical, functional line executives, not just staff. In this manner, a key line executive also had responsibility for a cross-functional process that his or her function depended heavily on.

As another example, when a major Asia-Pacific utility provider first attempted business process management, the ownership responsibilities were assigned to a headquarter's central staff that reported directly to the CEO. Their thinking was that a center of excellence would be required to apply the new business process management skills. The senior executives of the business units, however, subsequently ignored the new staff, and major process improvements were stifled. Additionally, they felt that although employees from the business units initially comprised the process management central staff, over time those people would no longer be in tune with the business realities of their former silos. In that company, the heads of each line of business had a history of not communicating or cooperating with one another. The culture was inward and silo focused and had succeeded in a protected monopolistic environment. However, when the country deregulated public utilities, the company was faced with a new dilemma: competition. As a result, CVM was added to their approach for business process management.

The first move made by the CVM expert was to coax the key executives out of their silo mentality. Each line executive was assigned responsibility for an enterprisewide customer-facing process or support process. To do this job right, each executive was dependent on his or her colleagues, whose functional areas were also participants in that process. Those other executives, in turn, were also codependent on one another, each for their own assigned processes. To become customer centered, the company first had to change the functional culture and management practices that were preventing effective cross-enterprise improvement.

The resources of the business (financial, I/T support staff, etc.) must be allocated to the business processes based on the voice of the customer. In other words, the contention for scarce resources within the company must be systematically resolved based on a horizontal view of the business, with the customer as the final arbiter. To become truly customer centered and preferred, the enterprise must view key assets and resources as a portfolio to be managed and expended to deliver an optimum, cross-functional value exchange to and from the external customer. Often, a major inhibitor to an organization realizing benefits from horizontal business process management is that the control of the investment dollars or scarce (e.g., I/T) resources of the business is left locked within the vertical silos. In these instances, process management will identify opportunities to improve the business but lack the wherewithal to implement them. Our experience with business transformation and major process reengineering is that the cross-functional improvement of an enterprise is heavily dependent on the ability to plan and allocate resources, such as I/T or funding, on a process basis. In the case of IBM, a super CIO position was ultimately created with overarching responsibility to drive enterprisewide business process improvement and to ensure an interlock with the critical I/T support resources.

Customer value management provides a mechanism to rationalize enterprisewide financial planning and resource allocation cross-functionally (and break up initiative gridlock) based on potential business returns from addressing customer needs. The foregoing subprocesses (Figure 9-1) comprise key elements of a definable, repeatable, ongoing process to monitor and meet the needs of a dynamic marketplace. One day after implementation of such an ongoing process, it is then possible to observe changes in the marketplace and maintain alignment between what the customers require and what the business is capable of delivering.

In Figure 9-2 this CVM process is presented in the context of the other enterprise processes. The figure depicts an ongoing CVM process as a primary input to the business plan and the other enterprise processes. In the example, a few of the generic processes are cited for a manufacturing enterprise. Customer value management spins off information that effectively uses the voice of the customer to validate or put into operation the company's business strategy and planning. Where the strategy targets specific customer segments, the outcomes of the required customer-facing processes are identified

A CVM Process Drives the Management System

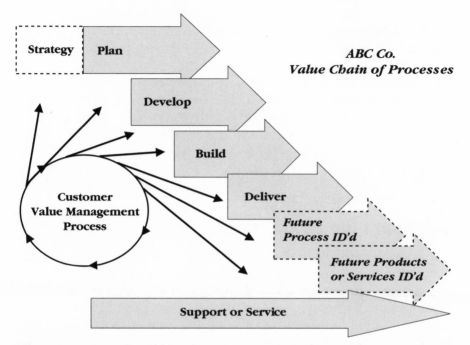

Figure 9-2 Using CVM to drive the enterprise: A manufacturing company example (© Copyright IBM, 1999)

along with the necessary design criteria to be capable of delivering customers' needs. Performance gaps, as identified by customers, are fed into the business plan, which in turn funds corrective measures and investments within the individual processes. In some cases, the analysis may indicate a requirement for a set of new business capabilities for which there are no existing processes and pinpoint where new formal processes should be established.

The company in Chapter 8 (Figure 8-6), for example, learned that many customers wanted to work with them directly rather than go through a channel intermediary. The capability to meet this need didn't exist, so the company had to design and implement a new process called direct access and a process for channel management to accommodate this new multiple channel environment. In this case, CVM provided the CEO with a mandate from the customers to create a new set of business capabilities and processes.

Another benefit of the management system in Figure 9-2 is that product development receives voice-of-the-customer input regarding business opportunities for new products and services. By linking CVM analyses to e-business channels, for example, customer buying patterns, complaints, and service requests (to name a few) may all be analyzed and provided to product managers real time. Hypotheses may be developed regarding newly emerging product and service opportunities. These can then be validated and expanded by conducting focus groups with customers to probe each hypothesized product or service and to develop segment-specific visions of ideal value delivery by the potential new offering.

Get the Full Benefits:
Automate the CVM Process

The CVM engine (Figure 9-2) for the business management system can be manually executed or automated. By adding technology to the process, more sophisticated and dynamic analyses can be conducted with a higher volume of data correlated and managed. Customer value management can then be more effectively and efficiently practiced as a combination of both qualitative and quantitative methods (i.e., focus groups followed by statistically valid surveys). Additional frameworks, such as quality function deployment (QFD) can make customer-focused business improvements significantly more quantitatively based. The more complex and broad the business scope, however, the greater the need for automating the analysis. Quality function deployment was discussed in Chapters 2 and 7 as a method to weight customer needs numerically and to align and link them to specific infrastructure investments. Techniques such as QFD provide a dramatic increase in management precision, and when coupled with the power of CVM they can create quite a challenge. The combined methods are so thorough that they tend to generate a great deal of actionable data and complexity. For example:

- The company may have many different customer segments, each with its own unique sets of needs for each interaction.
- The customers in each segment often interact with several different company processes and services.

- A single process has the potential for dozens of microinteractions for analysis to understand how value can be delivered to each of the segments.
- The customers, in turn, have many different needs and wants at each of the process microinteractions.
- Each of those needs have many corresponding process capability requirements, and each of those has very specific infrastructure requirements.
- And many of the infrastructure elements for a single given process capability also serve as prerequisites or enablers for other capabilities to meet other customer needs.

To determine the relative return on investment of a single piece of infrastructure (say, a new piece of telephone equipment), the business would need to understand:

- How many and which process capabilities would be enabled by this specific infrastructure investment?
- Which customer needs are directly impacted because of the capabilities being improved?
- What buying behaviors would be impacted if the company's performance of these customer needs improved?

  Are any of them basic must-have needs? Does the company performance of these needs currently fail to meet expectations? Will customers leave if performance of these needs is not improved?

  Are any of the needs differentiating attractors? Is the company currently lagging competition on the performance of these and subsequently losing share to the best provider?

  Are the customers with these needs high- or low-value customers?

- What are the relative costs versus return for this infrastructure item compared to the other infrastructure investments also being considered? (Again, for alternative infrastructure items, what capabilities are enabled and what customer needs are impacted?)

Analyzing and managing this myriad set of relationships are the types of complexities that lend themselves to automation. There are several versions of automated QFD on the market that are intended to help manufacturers manage similar complex interrelationships and dependencies. However, QFD was developed for product design, not for enterprisewide CVM and business process engineering.

IBM developed Dynamic Customer Value Management (DCVM), a patented automated tool designed specifically for customer-focused business process engineering. The intent was to enable a management team to focus on the results of an analysis of business improvement alternatives rather than on the mechanics of the analysis and the associated difficulty to identify, compile, and sort through all the variables. Automation enables management to see the results of a dynamic model of scenarios and to creatively model what-ifs such as: What would be the overall effect if we improve a particular factor by 10 percent?

Customer value management methods can be optimized through technologies such as DCVM, but such automation is not required to apply the concepts in this book. It merely makes the application more efficient. And in the case of designing or improving major corporatewide processes, DCVM makes the effort more practical. But the most compelling case for automation is the increase in precision and speed of investment decision making to determine the optimum business strategy in a chaotic marketplace (particularly when applied to model scenarios of rapidly changing market needs, such as today's e-business).

Automated DCVM takes changing marketplace input and effectively converts it to the business view (Figure 9-3). Automation of CVM often presents a highly advanced level of analysis in an easy to understand form, as in the figure. When a full-value analysis is conducted, the firm identifies many different variables that predict the potential benefit of each customer need on the business. The figure depicts how CVM can discern the relative business impact between many customer needs and then display that analysis on a single chart (whether done manually or assisted by automation). In this example, the customers of a business have identified six customer needs—depicted by letters A through F—which must be met during service interactions with a particular business process. (This is a rather simplified scenario. We more often deal with dozens of customer needs for a single process.)

Some of the needs in this example are basic must-have customer expectations, such as responsiveness or courtesy. For these basic needs, the customers' perception of the company's performance is plotted horizontally (left to right on the chart reflects low to high

Automated Dynamic CVM

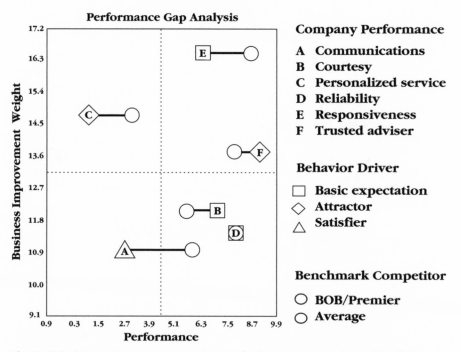

Figure 9-3 Converting a customer view to the business view: A model of business impact

performance) and is represented as a square. Company performance of attractor needs is plotted as a diamond, and satisfier needs are plotted as a triangle. This allows the management team to see how well (left to right axis) they are performing each company need as well as the behavior-driving impact of that need.

For more actionable information, the performance by competition of each need is also reflected. For the basic needs, the company is compared to the industry average performance, represented by open circles, as the company does not want to overinvest or try to become best of breed at basic needs. For attractors, which can differentiate a company and attract market share, however, the company is compared to the best competitor. Best competitor performance is depicted as a solid circle. And finally, company performance of satisfier category needs, which individually do not motivate buyer behavior, is compared to industry average performance.

The graphic allows the management team to discern quickly which of the needs occupy which buyer behavior category and then assess the company's performance versus the appropriate competition.

There is another critical message in Figure 9-3: the relative vertical placement of each of the customers' needs. This placement represents a company view of the relative weight and potential business impact of each need. The top most-sequenced need is the one that, if the company could focus only on a single need, would most benefit the business. The vertical placement corresponds to a numeric business improvement factor, or derived weighting, which considers the potential benefit of investing in each of the various customer needs. This vertical weighting of needs must be done for each target market segment and is the result of combining three factors to convert the market research from a customer view to a business view (this is more fully explained in Chapter 6):

- Customer importance weight, uplifted by
- Behavior-driver category (basic, satisfier, or attractor) weight, further uplifted by
- Competitive performance gap (percentage of gap between the company's performance and the industry average for basic and satisfier needs or the gap with best competitor for attractor needs).

As a result, a single graphic (Figure 9-3) converts the customer view into a company view. The vertical array of needs represents, in descending order, the sequence of customer needs which the business should potentially focus on if it could only address one, two, or three needs and so forth. With this approach, unmet basic needs (which threaten the business with loss of customers) will almost always appear as the top weighted opportunities for business improvement, followed by attractor needs, which lag the best competitor. It effectively answers a question commonly asked by senior management: Which are the critical few things that would most impact our business if they were improved? The depiction of both the vertical weightings and the horizontal comparison of gaps with competition effectively answers the executive's next question: Why?

Significantly, those vertical business improvement factor weights can be assigned not only to each customer need but also to their associated business capabilities and their infrastructure elements. In this manner, infrastructure investment recommendations from an automated CVM analysis are supported by corresponding weightings for each infrastructure item (depicting their relative business impact) plus a linkage back to the specific customer needs that are being enabled.

To better portray the power of these automated methods, the following figures will reflect the underlying architecture of the DCVM tool and its data management capabilities (Figures 9-4 and 9-5). While this can be done manually, the more complex the project or business scope, the more difficult that becomes.

This Is CVM Practiced at the PhD Level

When fully applied, CVM takes the customer-defined importance and performance levels of needs and wants and converts them to a business view of weighted opportunities for improvement. These

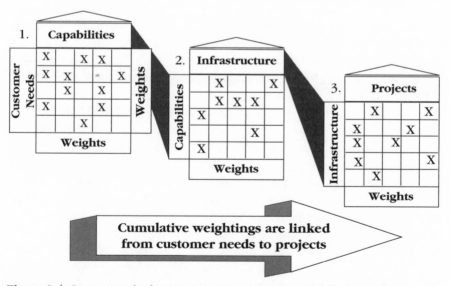

Aligning Customer Needs With Investments

Figure 9-4 Converting the business view to action: A model for improvement investments (© Copyright IBM, 1999)

weights ripple across the model (Figure 9-4) and are accumulated for each required business capability based on the number and weights of the customer needs that it provides and on to the required infrastructure elements based on the number and weightings of the capabilities that they support. Projects, in turn, are weighted as investment priorities based on the number and weights of the infrastructure elements that they provide. A major benefit here is that any project or infrastructure investment can be directly tied back to the customer need that it enables. When the investment is debated within the planning process, it can be supported with statements such as, "We must do this; it enables attainment of a basic customer need that we are currently not providing and which impacts customer loyalty and retention." Or in the case of an attractor need, "If we do this, 60 percent of the market surveyed said they would change vendors in order to get it."

An additional, but necessary, complexity is the assessment of the current presence or performance level for each of the capabilities and infrastructure elements. CPM pinpoints the business capabilities and infrastructure items that are both highly important and that are currently not performing well or are not present at all. Dynamic Customer Value Management is an automated means to capture and maintain an ongoing performance or presence assessment of each capability and infrastructure enabler. These may then be sorted and subsorted to provide a clearer picture of the capabilities and enablers that are currently missing (or performing at a relatively low level) and, among those, which would have the highest weight and business impact if improved (Figure 9-5).

The chart in Figure 9-5, reproduced from the DCVM automated tool, demonstrates an element of an automated analysis. The bottom portion of the graphic quickly identifies which business capabilities are the poorest performing and, within those, which ones have the greatest potential/weighting to improve the business. In this example, customer service has been analyzed for a firm, and several important process capabilities have been identified (the graphic contains only a partial set for illustrative purposes).

The Ns are business capabilities with no current presence. The Ls are present but with very low functionality or performance. Ms are those with medium functionality or performance. The Hs are those performing at the highest possible or desirable levels. After the sort,

Automated CVM

Capabilities clustered into
no, low, and medium presence...

- - - - - - - - - - - - - - - - -

and sorted,
within presence,
based on business
improvement weighting

		1 (CSR) can commit cross-functional resources	2 Manage critical path actitivies	3 Open for business 24 hours/7 days a week/365 days a year	4 Access to full customer relationship information	5 Access to information on all company products/services	6 Understands own company products/services	7 Understands own company organization and processes	8 Understands own company prices and contract T's and C's	9 Can capture customer issue for subsequent CSR to access	10 (CSR) networked with other knowledge workers	11 Understands competitors' products	12 Empowered to act within a range of authority	13 Communicates concern and empathy	14 Open 2 hours before/after 8 am to 5 pm	15 Provides multiple points of access	16 Provides toll-free telephone access	17 Understands customers' needs
		N	N	N	N	L	L	L	L	L	L	L	M	M	M	M	M	M
		1	2	3	4	5	6	7	8	9	10	11	12	13	14	15	16	17
Cumulative Weights	1	142	142	47	45	235	142	142	142	135	135	45	142	142	142	135	135	47
Normalized Weights	2	7	7	2	2	11	7	7	7	8	8	2	7	7	7	8	8	2
Pareto of Weights	3	1	2	3	4	5	6	7	8	9	10	11	12	13	14	15	16	17

Figure 9-5 Using automation to manage complexity: From data to decision making (© Copyright IBM, 1999)

the missing and low-performing capabilities (candidates for improvement) are apparent at the left of the chart.

Within each of the N L M H presence categories, the business capabilities have been subsorted in Figure 9-5 based on their relative potential to improve business performance. This is accomplished via a subsort within each N L M H category using their individual business improvement weights. Each capability links back to one or more customer needs, which were weighted earlier based on their potential for bottom-line business improvement. The Pareto chart at the bottom of the graphic identifies which of the capabilities offer the greatest business benefit by investing in their respective enabling infrastructure. The highest weighted capabilities that are categorized as N or L (not currently present or performing at a low level) become the top business improvement opportunities.

In CVM, once the necessary business capabilities to deliver customer needs have been identified, assessed, weighted, and prioritized, the infrastructure items necessary for each capability are also identified, assessed for presence, weighted, and prioritized.

When the final matrix in Figure 9-4 clusters infrastructure into projects and actions, the basis for a sound business case (return on investment) for each project is firmly established and documented. And the DCVM tool will also generate an automated Pareto analysis for the infrastructure items as well as the projects, similar to the capabilities assessment in Figure 9-5. The automated model can be dynamic and adjusted by modifying the customer-defined weights or performance metrics. For example, the management team can experiment with scenarios or projections of future market conditions such as the impact of a new entrant into the market or the introduction of a new technology that changes customer expectations and behavior drivers.

Walking the Talk at Bank X. A CVM analysis for a major North American bank established a set of improvement priorities for their customer service organization. Within the priorities, market research indicated that personalized service was a potential attractor and differentiator, particularly for smaller corporate customers. However, several of the more critical basic needs were not being performed well because the bank was experiencing severe administrative performance issues and control problems. As a result, the initial assessment was that the bank should postpone an investment in personalized service and focus on the critical must-have needs that were severely broken. If the bank did not address these, it would lose customers. However, by modeling future scenarios, such as a major additional merger within one year that would make the control issues even worse, personalized service became a critical success factor, not a nice-to-have market attractor. Prior to the merger, there would not be time to put self-editing and correcting business processes completely into place to address their current control issues. Other processes, although currently working well, would also be put under stress, causing even more to fail. In this dynamic scenario, personalized service could be expected to change in importance to become a basic must-have need. Customers of the acquired bank, faced with new vendor practices and procedures (compounded by broken support processes), would expect their bank to provide an extraordinary level of personal assistance. The extent to which they could provide personalized service would determine the bank's capability to retain customers over the dynamic short-term postmerger time frame.

So, utilizing a DCVM approach, the management team did a manual intervention to the weightings, envisioned their postmerger scenario, and projected personalized service to become, in effect, an unmet basic need. This modeling moved that requirement to the top of the business view of weighted customer needs. The capabilities to meet that need and the related infrastructure items were uplifted in importance accordingly. A new model was generated of recommended projects which accounted for the dynamic business environment and correctly reflected the company view rather than only the raw customer research data. The subsequent business improvement projects contained an appropriate blend of actions to address all of the currently broken must-have needs, but with a special emphasis on actions that would also anticipate dynamic environment.

Automation of the management system with Dynamic CVM makes such an analysis practical. It also enables an ongoing process to monitor and refresh the business vision continuously as the marketplace experiences introductions of new technology (e.g., the Internet) and as customer expectations are continuously reset. Critical process performance improvements or new infrastructure requirements are quickly identified and funded. The ability to sense and respond to changing market conditions becomes a core business competency so that, one day later, the business continues to be aware of and maintain alignment with the views of customers.

Arriving at that enviable position requires a customer-focused evolution, if not a revolution, that is best characterized as a journey, which we discuss in more detail in Chapter 10. And maintaining that position is a never-ending journey.

EXERCISE
Applying CVM to Your Business

Management Issues

How do you institutionalize being a customer-centered enterprise? How do you make customer value analyses an ongoing part of your management system and the fabric of your business? How do you maintain an alignment with customers once you have attained it?

- Is being a customer-centered enterprise formalized into ongoing processes to monitor changing customer and market perceptions and to drive business strategy, planning, and investments?

- Do you have a horizontal, cross-enterprise, customer-focused management system?

- Do process owners have authority to represent the external customer and set cross-silo functional improvement priorities?

- Are the key assets and resources (i.e., I/T staff or financial) allocated cross-functionally based on targeted external customers' needs and wants?

- Are infrastructure investments prioritized based on formal processes that convert a customer view to a business view of improvement opportunities?

- Do you capitalize on automation to dynamically model scenarios of changing market conditions and business improvement and investment priorities?

- Is customer transaction data captured, mined, and harvested as a source of market intelligence to drive ongoing microsegmentation, targeted marketing, and personalized customer service?

- As change occurs in the marketplace, will you be one day out of sync tomorrow? Or will you quickly sense and respond to (or predict) those changes?

10

The Journey

A Customer-Focused Evolution

"Why are we using first names? I don't want to be your friend. I just want some breakfast."
MICHAEL DOUGLAS, AS AN IRATE CUSTOMER,
TO A FAST-FOOD RESTAURANT MANAGER IN
THE MOVIE *FALLING DOWN*

My favorite airline sent me a letter of invitation to use the Internet to book my next flight. The cheapest airfare was promised along with an additional $25 off for booking electronically. When I tried to use their new Web page, it required an extensive enrollment process so they could get customer information for their database. Ostensibly, the airline was going to get "close to me" by gathering a great deal of market intelligence while delighting me with their inside-out view of superior service. After 45 minutes, however, I was still laboring to book a flight, as I was completely unable to navigate their (e-access) Web site. Ultimately, I called their telephone reservations center and made my reservation, angry at having to pay a $25 premium for giving them my business by phone. Another effort by a product-centric company to become a customer-centered organization had gone awry. Good intentions on their part, but poor execution.

The business world today is characterized by such an intense, and often disorganized, desire to become more customer centered. Virtually every major corporation is grappling with how to develop and implement strategies, plans, and programs to move closer to their customers. The content and scope (and effectiveness) of these plans can

219

vary wildly, however, based on the strategic intent of each organization and its current starting point. Perhaps your company has recognized the issues discussed in this book and is looking to make the firm more attractive to a target market. As we will discuss, your capabilities to be customer centered must be developed as part of a journey, and the questions are: Where are you today? Where do you want to be?

Where Are You Now? First You Must Walk Before You Can Run

Your starting point may be a heavily internal and product-focused culture. Product-focused companies are characterized by market approaches that tend to lever their internal strengths, such as a strong research and development capability or a proprietary technology. IBM was incredibly successful during the early years of computing as a highly product-centric company. IBM's focus on product research, development, and manufacturing provided such great customer benefit that the firm's organization and cultural alignment centered around its technology and the products that technology generated. That certainly isn't unique. Many product-centric companies successfully lever such a focus in the marketplace, but only as long as the customer sees a differentiating value in those products or is highly dependent on them. However, once that differentiating product value or dependency is no longer recognized, the advantage can disappear.

Companies like Microsoft, with a single mass-production and mass-marketing value proposition, may feel little compelling need to become more customer oriented or to develop the ability to meet the needs of a segment of one customer. (Just try ordering a fast-food burger without the special sauce, and you'll see what I mean.) As a result, a heavily product-focused business will often have similar capabilities in its business processes. Product-focused manufacturing companies, for example, often also have mass-marketing or macromarket-segment-focused marketing and service capabilities. Since they lack the ability to manufacture a tailored, customer-specific product, they seldom have (and for a time period may not need) data regarding individual customer needs, wants, or preferences. Often these companies, such as automobile manufacturers, also rely heavily on a channel, which puts them even further apart from customers and from information about the actual customer. Those are truly distribution channels for pushing a product out to a consumer. As a result, when such a company comes under pressure to migrate from a product focus to a customer focus (say, a large utility that is deregulated and suddenly has competitors), its starting point is a major issue. For such a firm, even the ability to segment the customer base crudely into a few large groupings with similar needs and wants becomes a major undertaking.

Segmentation of customers would require some basic, but missing, capabilities and enabling infrastructure, such as a database of the customers (and prospective customers). A history of all sales and service interactions would have to exist in the company's records by customer name. Or segmentation might be done via questionnaires to the customer, but that would require an organization with the skills to accomplish that or to manage subcontracting and analysis of the effort. Once the customer segments are known and their needs understood, the business would need multiple (modular) process capabilities to do things in different ways for the different customer segments. In addition, the infrastructure would need to exist (procedures, training, measurements, rewards, information, technology, etc.) to support those capabilities.

Of course, employees' attitudes would need to change, too. Otherwise, employees of a utility service provider would continue to refer to customers as "meters." The company would have new round processes but a square culture.

With such a product-centered starting point, a leap from no segmentation at all (completely past segment-focused services) to one-to-one personalized service would be monumental. Basic business capabilities must come first simply to recognize that "one size does not fit all." First you must walk (have the ability to develop and produce a standardized, consistent product or service), next you can run (have the ability to do this several different ways to attract and meet the needs of several different groups or segments of people), and then you can consider moving on to flight (expand that capability to give each person exactly what they want, when and how they want it). That progression of business capabilities represents positions on a customer-focused maturity curve (Figure 10-1) that firms can either occupy or progress through.

Our research and cross-industry experience have shown that many companies are successful when they target and stake out a market-dominant position on the curve depicted in Figure 10-1. Some companies are product centered and bring value to the market based on their unique product development or manufacturing capabilities; others are customer centered and bring value based on their ability to understand and meet the needs of customers (either market segments or individual customers).

Companies such as AT&T, Microsoft, and Toyota are arguably product centric and have profitably leveraged their research, development, and manufacturing capabilities to stake out a strong leadership position in the marketplace. Their business strategies are focused on maintaining and differentiating themselves at this position.

Other more market-segment-centric companies have achieved success by targeting specific clusters of potential customers who have common needs or values and by providing a product or service that more closely matches the desires of that segment. Volvo and Mercedes, for example, have a tightly focused view of the marketplace and compete by offering very specific value propositions to well-defined customer segments. And while the Toyota brand has succeeded with a more product-focused mass appeal, their Lexus brand has staked out and is excelling at a more targeted market-segment-focused position on the customer-maturity curve.

The Journey: From Product- to Customer-Centered

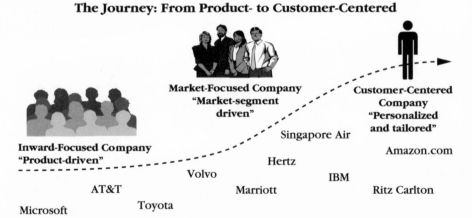

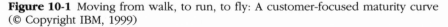

Figure 10-1 Moving from walk, to run, to fly: A customer-focused maturity curve (© Copyright IBM, 1999)

Still others, such as Motorola (with personalized pagers), Levis (with custom jeans), and Ritz Carlton (with organizational memory of an individual customer's preferences), have moved to occupy a segment of one space on the customer-focused maturity curve. And the Fidelity.coms and Schwab.coms and Amazon.coms of the Internet have set their sights to differentiate themselves further by providing an unprecedented level of personalized products and services. Collectively, all of these customer-centered companies are setting new thresholds for customer intimacy. The needs and values of their individual customers determine the actual product or service delivered at key moments of truth interactions.

Where Do You Want to Be? Walk? Run? Fly?

In each of these examples, the company has staked out and has become highly proficient at competing at a specific position on the curve. However, whether a company has successfully captured a position or not, all businesses today are faced with a critical strategic decision: Where must I be on the curve in the future? Given the dynamic changes that are taking place in the world of commerce (totally new e-business capabilities; rampant restructuring of industries; dramatic increases in tailored, personalized service; rapidly rising customer expectations and highly volatile economies), no one can feel secure. Today, the compelling issue for a successful company that is currently skewed toward the middle or left of the curve is whether that position is sustainable over time. And the less successful competitor must look beyond the current positioning of the industry leaders toward a new vision—the next plateau for that group—and strive to "shoot ahead of the competitive ducks."

For virtually all companies, the issues are both their current starting point and the desired end state on the customer-maturity curve. And here is where we close the loop in our discussion of CVM and tie back to some key statements in Chapter 1:

- Every company has a mission and vision statement.
- In today's world, that mission and vision must consider and often will include the word *customer.*

- To fulfill or operationalize that vision, new management methods such as CVM are required to enable a firm to become customer centered.

However, the firm must decide where it wants to be on the customer-focused (centered) maturity curve. The customers must be targeted and their needs and wants understood either as a mass-consumer market (product focus), as needs-based market segments, or as segments of one. Then, given the customer view obtained via CVM methods, the desired position on the maturity curve must be attained by deploying specific required process capabilities and enabling infrastructure throughout the firm.

Where Do Your Customers Want You to Be? This Will Vary by Customer Segment

When a company desires to move from a product focus to a customer-centered focus, it must pick its destination on the customer-maturity curve. The company vision, mission, and strategy may have a center of gravity around being customer centered, or customer focused, meaning understanding and meeting the needs of target market segments. Or the firm may strive to be close to the customer by being individual customer centered, meaning segments of one. Phrases such as micromarketing or one-to-one customer relationships are often embedded into the internal communications and strategies of such companies with little means for making them realities. Customer intimacy is now the battle cry of organizations. It may be a battle cry, but the managers and employees of companies using that term frequently struggle to define it and to find ways of accomplishing that elusive (and ill-defined) goal.

Big Teleco: Making the Customer-Centered Connection.　I was conducting executive interviews at the headquarters of one of Asia's largest telephone companies, where the CEO had recently proclaimed customer intimacy to be their second highest strategic goal. (I imagine the top goal had something to do with products or revenue.) An executive who reported to the CEO confided, "No one here actually knows what customer intimacy is. More importantly, no one knows what it isn't. So, as a result, every financial proposal from every department in the company is now labeled a customer-intimacy initiative!" Their quandary was that they had no way to identify and prioritize the investments required to attain a business goal that had no clear definition. In this scenario, $50,000 for paint to restripe the parking lot could be touted as a customer-intimacy initiative.

So what is customer intimacy? As the telephone company executive said, "Ask any number of our employees, and that is how many different definitions you will get." He added that those opinions, though diverse, were also passionately held and often the subject of intense debate. It sounded familiar, especially when I recalled the internal debates that went on within IBM while trying to define who the customer was.

What this company had was a classic case of a firm currently positioned at the far left of the customer-maturity curve depicted in Figure 10-1, with an objective to arrive at an end state on the far right. Although companies have excelled in the past at a single position on the curve, the majority of the firms I speak with today are trying to move across the spectrum from being product focused to becoming a customer-centered enterprise. Some will stop at the point of understanding and servicing their market segments, whereas others have the goal or objective to provide tailored, personalized value delivery at the individual-customer level.

It may sound trite, but the real answer to the question, "What is customer intimacy?" is whatever your customers define it to be. You must decide whom you want to be your targeted customers. These targeted customers must decide what would constitute ideal interactions with you and what level of intimacy or personalized knowledge-based delivery of value they desire.

Today, those customers' definition of ideal interactions will vary greatly by industry. Customers generally desire a wide range of product alternatives from financial service providers, with flexibility to meet very personalized individual needs. However, those same customers generally accept a narrower band of alternatives or personalization from automobile manufacturers or airlines to get the lower price associated with mass production. It also varies greatly within an industry: Some financial services customers want a financial adviser who has an intimate knowledge of them and understands their personal situation and goals, whereas other customers make up self-sufficient segments that do not want advice. In many such instances, ideal customer-defined intimacy is no intimacy at all. Certain bank customers in CVM value-visioning focus groups have said, "I don't want to have to be pleasant or be nice or to have them know me. I just want my bank balance. Let me get it by pushing a few buttons on the phone." For that segment, the answer to the question of what customer intimacy is would clearly differ from some other customers.

Customer value management allows a company to identify exactly how customer centered they should be from the point of view of each customer. This enables you to form segments of customers with a common view on whether or not you should have intimate knowledge of them for personalized value delivery. As Michael Douglas's character said after reading the fast-food manager's nametag in the movie *Falling Down*, "Why are we using first names? I don't want to be your friend. I just want some breakfast." Customer intimacy had gone beyond the needs of the targeted customer and had become a driver of dissatisfaction.

Where You Want to Be Will Also Vary by Each Business Process

Once a company has identified what kind of enterprise it wants to be, it must still determine whether each process should optimally be product, segment, or individual-customer focused. As surprising as this may seem, the level of customer centeredness should be considered process by process (Figure 10-2).

For example, Motorola exhibits some capabilities to suggest that they gain benefits from applying the curve differently at different points in their business. (Note: This is not to suggest that these are all of their capabilities for those processes or that they do not have additional capabilities for different business objectives or particular segments.)

- Mass-marketing processes may be very practical for a company such as Motorola, particularly when the marketing message is that "we can do it your way, personalized and individualized."

A successful enterprise may have different processes at different positions on the curve.

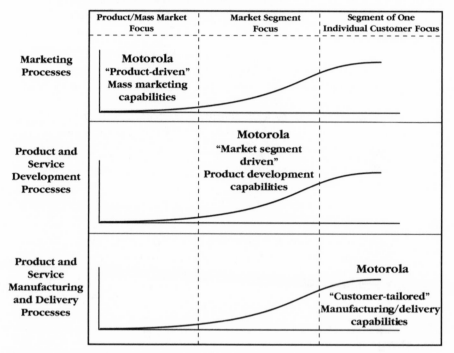

Figure 10-2 Applying the maturity curve: Process by process (© Copyright IBM, 1999)

- Their product development processes, on the other hand, are clearly able to identify highly profitable market segments (both commercial and consumer) and then develop appropriately strong value propositions into their product line.

- The manufacturing and delivery processes, however, are capable of millions of product permutations and can literally deliver an individualized, personalized product (within those permutations) that is close to a personally tailored product, but with the cost efficiency of mass production.

The point is that a firm can have a center of gravity and a competitive advantage around a position on the curve (Motorola is renowned for personalized, segment of one, product delivery); however, all processes do not have to be at that same point.

Additionally, for some firms, benefits are gained by having multiple process capabilities for the same process, allowing them to lever multiple positions on the curve for that process (Figure 10-3). The figure depicts how a firm, such as British Airways, may design multiple capabilities into a single process to accomplish multiple objectives. In the case of BA, the manufacturing and delivery processes for products and services display some capabilities to perform well at all three positions on the curve. For example:

- *Mass-market or product-focused manufacturing and delivery.* British Airways successfully delivers a very common product to a mass market including standardized seats, routes, and airplane designs for all customers. The focus here is on delivering a high-quality, commonly accepted product. Certain standardized services are also provided to customers in general, such as baggage handling.

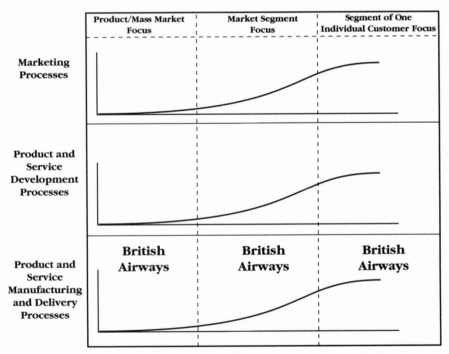

A process may be modular and need competitive capabilities for different points on the curve.

Figure 10-3 Applying the maturity curve: Across a single process (© Copyright IBM, 1999)

- *Market-segment-focused manufacturing and delivery*. However, BA customers have also been segmented based on their relative value to the airline, and the company's product and service delivery processes deliver an appropriate, highly differentiated, greater level of value to customers who occupy these different value-based segments. (Airlines typically identify these segments with correlating tiered symbols of value, such as Bronze, Silver, Gold, and Platinum frequent flyers.) As a result, these targeted high-value customers receive increased levels of products and services such as executive lounges, special counters for express check-in, preboarding the airplane, and courtesy upgrades to first-class service with larger seats, special meals, and free drinks.

  These same amenities are also available to the lower value customers (lower level or nonfrequent fliers) but at an additional or tiered price. This tiered pricing, based on the value-based segment the customer occupies, maintains the balance of value provided to and value received from their customers. In this manner, airlines such as BA avoid spraying the customer base with undifferentiated high-cost services without regard to the value of the customer.

- *Individualized, personalized, segment of one focused manufacturing and delivery*. British Airways can also take its product and service delivery down to the individual level. Individual preferences are met (within the value-based segment the customer occupies to maintain profitability) in areas such as assuring that seating preferences and dietary needs are identified and provided.

Thus, BA is able to provide an array of products and services that satisfy multiple business objectives and market needs which cross the spectrum of mass market, market segment, and individual-customer focus (Figure 10-3). Figure 10-4 moves from a single vendor analysis, such as British Airways, to multiple vendors. It depicts how different firms may successfully compete in the same generic market space (e.g., airlines) but occupy dramatically different positions on the customer curve. This is because their target market requires very different business capabilities. For example, there will always be customers who value price beyond all else. However, targeting a market that values lowest price does not mean that CVM is not required. The needs and wants identified will simply be different than those of segments that value and benefit from differentiated products and services. In the case of the low-cost-focused consumer, as targeted by Southwest and

Within an industry or market, different companies may compete successfully from different positions.

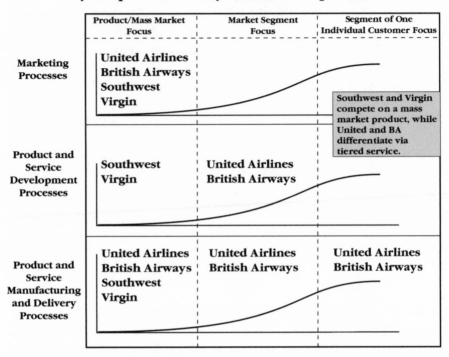

	Product/Mass Market Focus	Market Segment Focus	Segment of One Individual Customer Focus
Marketing Processes	United Airlines British Airways Southwest Virgin		*Southwest and Virgin compete on a mass market product, while United and BA differentiate via tiered service.*
Product and Service Development Processes	Southwest Virgin	United Airlines British Airways	
Product and Service Manufacturing and Delivery Processes	United Airlines British Airways Southwest Virgin	United Airlines British Airways	United Airlines British Airways

Figure 10-4 Applying the maturity curve: Within an industry (© Copyright IBM, 1999)

Virgin, their basic needs (other than price) must still be identified and provided, albeit on a more generic, mass basis. So for these airlines, their marketing, product development, and product and service manufacturing and delivery are done as low-cost, mass-production processes to provide what the customers value most: low price.

It's a Journey

For a firm to occupy any position on the curve successfully requires several distinct business capabilities and their associated infrastructure (as depicted by their particular CVM pyramid), which are cumulative and therefore a journey (Figure 10-5). To be market segment focused requires major capabilities and infrastructure to capture and analyze

The Journey: a unique "mix" of *current vs. desired* business capabilities across the different processes of the enterprise.

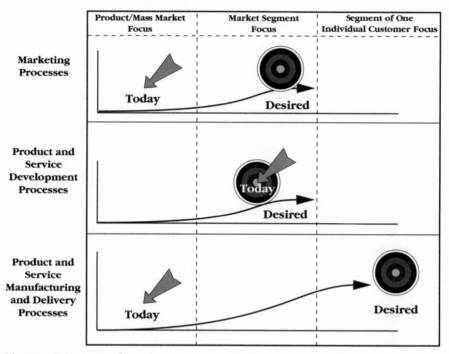

Figure 10-5 Moving from the current state to the target state: The journey (© Copyright IBM, 1999)

data regarding groupings of customers, to understand their needs and their current or future value to the company, and to respond accordingly with the appropriate product or services at the points of interaction. And to provide individualized services to segments of one, the foregoing becomes even more granular and a further step on the journey with customer-specific transaction and preference data captured, analyzed, and subsequently accessed at the point of (personalized) service delivery for each individual customer.

Customer value management is a methodical approach that enables a company to fulfill its vision of becoming the premier provider to its targeted customers. It can be applied at the level of an individual process or service or on an enterprisewide basis to attain an optimum mix of different levels of customer focus for different business processes (Figure 10-5). The journey across the curve tends to be an evolution, as a product-focused or mass-market-focused firm cannot simply leap to provide individualized service without some prerequisite segment-based capabilities. The scope and scale of that journey, however, can no longer be simply expressed as mere process reengineering. To become customer centered requires a firm to go beyond reengineering to business transformation and to a management system that is driven by the customer view (Figure 10-6).

A closed-loop customer relationship management system for customer focus and organizational learning is depicted in Figure 10-6. One may enter into this model at any point to discuss it. For this discussion, the most logical is at the point of "Customers." As the graphic depicts, customer data are captured at the point of interaction with key processes (their profile, preferences, and transaction data) and retained in a customer database. The data are analyzed for purposes of:

- Segmentation to monitor changing value-based or needs-based segments of customers and to target them.

- Current and future profit analysis to determine which customers warrant higher cost, differentiating service levels versus providing the low-value customers with only low-cost services that meet their basic needs).

- Risk analysis to minimize exposure to bad debts.

- Attrition projection to forecast and predict potential defectors and take action to save them.

- Propensity to buy the next product to enable targeted marketing campaigns as well as tailored cross-sell offerings during customer service interactions.

- Personalized service delivery to enable customer-facing personnel to respond appropriately and provide cost-effective (e.g., based on value of the customer) differentiating (e.g., based on preferences of the customer) service delivery.

The next major point in the management system depicted in Figure 10-6 is an ongoing process for CVM to:

- Monitor changing needs and values by target market segment.

- Monitor changing customer perceptions of company performance and competitive gaps.

- Identify customer-defined improvement priorities.
- Input business improvements and investment plans.
- Monitor and measure results.

This is followed by business process management to:

- Identify core business processes that cross organizations and functions.

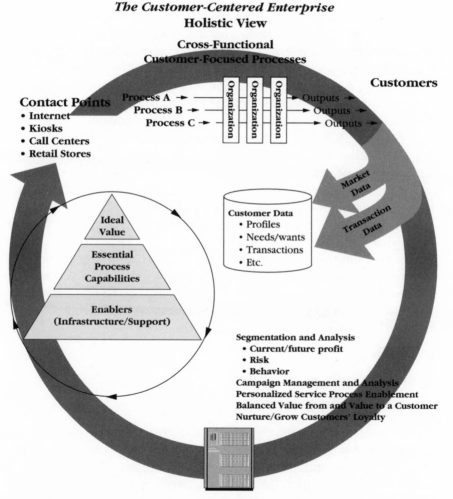

Figure 10-6 The end state: CVM and customer relationship management (© Copyright IBM, 1999)

- Implement process improvements and investments that are customer driven and based on CVM input.

- Execute processes that are customer-data-driven, including "snapping in" modular process capabilities at the point of service delivery that are based on knowledge of segment (or segment of one) needs and wants. Ensure that marketing, sales, and service execution are driven by segment- or customer-specific values.

In turn, this results in process outcomes at transaction touch points with customers (back to the customer starting point in Figure 10-6) that are exactly what the customer wants and are captured and retained in a customer database for analysis and repeat of the cycle. Such a cycle is self-correcting and adjusts to a changing marketplace and changing customer needs and priorities. Each cycle of this customer-centered management system brings the firm progressively closer to the customer to fulfill the customer-focused vision. It also fulfills a business vision to attract, retain, and develop profitable customers.

Customer value management and being customer centered are a way of thinking and running a business or organization. It is as simple or as complex as being able to determine whom you want as a customer, identify what it is that will attract and satisfy them, and then give it to them. It manages the execution by assuring that the capabilities of the business to deliver value are aligned with the things that customers value and that drive their behavior. It assures those capabilities by aligning the required processes, organization, incentives, measures, rewards, and technology with those customer-defined design points. And as depicted in Figure 10-6, it enables a closed-loop management system to establish and execute a winning strategy for customer loyalty and growth.

Beyond Customer Intimacy: The e-Revolution

The pressure for a company to become customer centered and to move from left to right on the customer-maturity curve will only increase as more and more consumers become accustomed to doing business on the Internet. It is somewhat analogous to our earlier discussion that attractors inevitably become basic customer needs and expectations. As affordable Internet access continues to rise, through a multiplicity of low-cost devices and channels and a proliferation of Web sites with sophisticated and secure transaction capabilities, so will adoption rates increase among consumers and businesses. The rise in usage will quickly incent more companies to use the Internet strategically and tactically to reach the growing market. For customers faced with a potpourri of personalized choices and enabled by ease of access to new vendors with better "deals," intimacy and loyalty will take on a whole new meaning. Buying behavior will be influenced not only by what customers experience at a company's site but also through affiliate's networks, chat rooms, reverse auctions, and other communities of interest that they encounter on popular portal sites. The old axiom that "a dissatisfied customer will tell seven others in the neighborhood" no longer applies. With the power of the Internet, it is now a global neighborhood, and a dissatisfied customer will have the power to tell seven million others.

Confronted with these realities, a business today has no choice but to intensify and accelerate the ability to understand market and customer needs, including who is setting their expectations with the speed of an Internet transaction, and to respond accordingly. Today's customer intimacy is tomorrow's expected quality. However, by integrating CVM into your business approach and management system, you stand a good chance of controlling your own destiny. You can set the expectations bar that others will have to meet. You can provide the high-value experience at each customer interaction that will attract and retain customers. And when combined with e-business capabilities such as smart agents, data mining, and network-based technologies, you can improve on it live, in Web time, so that every transactional experience can be better than the last one.

It's now up to you. The company that fully levers the potential of CVM will become ideally customer centered and attain its vision to become the premier provider to its customers. Your competitors are now reading this book! So are your customers. What is your customer's vision of an ideal you? How will you execute it?

EXERCISE
Applying CVM to Your Business

Management Issues

Where on the customer-maturity curve do you wish to be as a business enterprise? What are the implications for your individual processes? What is your starting point and what must change to reach the target end state?

- What is your current enterprise center of gravity in relation to a customer-focused maturity curve?

- Where are your current key competitors on the curve?

- Are you targeting the same segments as key competitors? Should you be targeting them?

- Where on the curve do you need to be in one to three years?

- Where do your target customers want you to be? How "intimate" do they want you to be?

- What are your key business processes? Where are they positioned on the curve today?

- Where must they be, individually, to collectively attain your desired enterprise end state?

- How will the Internet affect rising customer expectations? How can you be the one who sets those expectations?

Acknowledgments

During the course of our journey, we have developed customer value management by meeting and working with some of the world's leading innovators in the management sciences, including:

Dr. Michael Hammer, the author of the *Harvard Business Review* article "Don't Automate, Obliterate" and the best-selling books *Reengineering the Corporation* and *Beyond Reengineering*. Dr. Hammer's process reengineering methods provided an initial platform for breakthrough thinking, which we built on by developing advanced voice-of-the-customer visioning methods for our own customer-driven business improvement and redesign approaches.

Dr. Gary Hamel, whose advice, books, and *Harvard Business Review* articles on strategic intent and core competencies greatly influenced our decision to position CVM as a core competency for customer-focused business reengineering within IBM and also as a cornerstone for our external client management consulting.

Dr. Robert Camp, author of the then groundbreaking *Harvard Business Review* article "How to Measure Yourself Against the Best" and best-selling book *Bench marking: The Search for Industry Best Practices That Lead to Superior Performance*. After meeting and colecturing with Dr. Camp, innovative new approaches were developed to make our own benchmarking methods uniquely customer focused. These were subsequently used in successful benchmarking relationships between IBM and other process-focused companies.

Dr. N. Akao, whose quality function deployment (QFD) approaches revolutionized the .art and science of using the voice of the customer for product design and inspired the classic *Harvard Business Review* article, "House of Quality." These concepts, developed originally for the "hard" processes in manufacturing, provided us with valuable insights on how to use CVM to design "soft" administrative business processes and services that align with customer needs and values.

Dr. Valarie Zeithaml, Dr. Leonard Berry, and Dr. A. Parasuraman, whose extensive research on customer service and customer satisfaction management and whose book, *Delivering Quality Service: Balancing Customer Perceptions and Expectations*, have become the basis for what is now widely implemented as "Servqual." A portion of IBM CVM focuses on identifying and meeting the expectations of customers. The diagnostics and prescriptives cited by Dr. Zeithaml and associates provided a simple framework to meet basic customer expectations and manage dissatisfaction.

Dr. Noriaki Kano, Science University of Tokyo, whose research and conclusions regarding "attractive quality" provided insights and inspiration for our development of powerful new management disciplines that use buyer behaviors to prioritize business improvements. Whereas Dr. Zeithaml and her associates provided a framework to meet customer expectations, Dr. Kano called out the potential to identify both basic expectations and also the critical few additional needs that could differentiate a firm and attract market share. If customer needs and wants could be categorized into their basic needs (which prevent attrition) and attractors/differentiators (which drive increased share), we reasoned that aligning business capabilities with these needs categories would result in customer-centered retention or growth. The other customer needs that do not fall into either of these behavior-driving categories could be eliminated from the business design (and reduce costs).

Dr. John Henderson of the Massachusetts Institute of Technology and Boston University, whose concepts of "strategic alignment," and of linking infrastructure to the process capabilities they enable, provided a rational basis to identify and quantify information technology (I/T) value. By combining concepts such as Dr. Akao's quality function deployment with Dr. Henderson's research and findings on defining the infrastructure that drives desired process results, CVM was moved from concept to practice. Customer value management could be done continuously as an ongoing process in its own right.

Dr. Michael Shank (now of IBM) and colleagues Dr. Bart Victor and Dr. Andrew Boynton of the International Institute for Managment Development, Lausanne, Switzerland. Their research and publications for IBM on Dynamic Stability and the Business Transformation Strategic Framework provided a means to define and align a firm's desired market positioning and the associated business capabilities, that is, those required for invention, mass production, continuous improvement, or mass customization. Customer value management has become an ideal management vehicle to operationalize such concepts because it secures a customer and marketplace definition regarding which of these should be the firm's target market position and then identifies the specific business capabilities required.

Dr. B. Joseph Pine II, whose book *Mass Customization, The New Frontier in Business Competition* (written while he was a colleague at IBM) provided the framework to envision how CVM could be used to develop a customer view of one-to-one, personalized service delivery and to design the modularized process capabilities required to implement that vision.

Executives, managers, and employees of the IBM Corporation, who transformed the company from a highly centralized, product-focused organization and culture to a decentralized, customer-centered company. The subsequent business process cost reduction (over $7 billion), while improving customer satisfaction and stockholder value (tenfold), are testimony to the power and potential benefits of customer-centric business process management and capabilities engineering.

Client CEOs and senior management of *Fortune 100* and *Global 1000* corporations, who have utilized our CVM approaches to become customer centered and drive growth in a rapidly changing world where customers have become kings and queens and management as usual has become a threat to continued business success. Working with these client businesses has provided a laboratory for the development of what we know today are the best practices globally in customer-focused business improvement.

Joe Diorio, who patiently coached and assisted a novice writer.

My friends and colleagues Vin Pizzo, Ed Murphy, Mike Shank, Jim Cortada, and Colin Livingstone, who have helped me over the years and most recently took time from busy schedules to review the manuscript and provide their insights and constructive criticism. Thank you, all.

Harvey Thompson

Index

About the Author

Harvey Thompson is the IBM Global Executive for Customer Value Management Consulting. As corporate program director, he led the development and deployment of innovative, customer-focused business process improvement approaches that have been used successfully within IBM and Fortune 500 and Global 1000 companies worldwide. Thompson is a lecturer at the Advanced Business Institute in New York as well as the International Executive Education Centers in Brussels, Belgium, and Milan, Italy. He is a frequent speaker at professional conferences on the topics of CVM and Customer Loyalty Management and his articles have been featured in publications such as the *Journal of Business Strategy*. He can be contacted at HThompson@customer-centered-ent.com.